Principles of Employment Law

Principles of Employment Law

Denis Keenan, LLB(Hons),FCIS,DMA,CertEd
of the Middle Temple, Barrister-at-Law

Formerly Head of Department of Business Studies and Law,
Mid-Essex Technical College and School of Art
(now the Chelmer Institute of Higher Education)

Anderson Keenan Publishing

First published 1979

Anderson Keenan Publishing Ltd
53 Great Sutton Street
London EC1V 0DQ

© Denis Keenan 1979

ISBN: 0 906501 05 9 cased
      0 906501 04 0 paper

Typeset by Columns
Printed and bound in Great Britain by
The Garden City Press Limited, Letchworth,
Hertfordshire SG6 1JS.

Contents

Preface

This book is intended primarily for students who must have a knowledge of Employment Law for the purpose of qualifying in a profession where law, though essential in terms of the working environment, is not a subject which the student, having qualified, will be required to practise in the narrow sense. Thus those studying for the examinations of the Association of Certified Accountants, the Institute of Cost and Management Accountants, and the Institute of Chartered Secretaries and Administrators may, for example, find the book useful.

It could also be used on courses in universities and colleges leading to internal awards of many kinds where the course has a mainly practical content rather than a highly theoretical one.

Those in business who require an overview of the subject or parts of it but have neither the time nor the need to go very deeply into it because it is not their main function, may also find the book to be of use.

The intention has been to write a book which is not overlong but which nevertheless manages to deal adequately with major principles. Most of those who use it, whether they are students or in business, will already have completed courses of study at 'A' level and degree level which it is hoped will have developed thought processes and opened windows in minds. However, when using this book they will be seeking to equip themselves to begin a working life in a practical environment. If this book is of some assistance in that regard it will have achieved the purpose for which it was written.

Finally, I would like to thank my wife, Mary, for preparing the typescript and the indexes to cases and statutes. Any errors and omissions are, of course, my fault.

Denis Keenan   September 1979

1 The Relationship of Employer and Employee

Employment law is based upon the relationship of employer and employee (or in older terminology, master and servant), and it is therefore important to consider first how this relationship is established and what the general legal consequences are.

THE CONTRACT OF EMPLOYMENT

In normal circumstances there is no difficulty in establishing the relationship of employer and employee since there is available an overwhelming amount of evidence that a contract of employment exists. The employee has been selected by the employer and works full-time under some form of supervision for a wage or salary. The employer deducts income tax from the wage or salary under PAYE arrangements, makes Social Security contributions and often provides a pension scheme for the employee. In addition, although the contract need not be in writing, s. 1 of the Employment Protection (Consolidation) Act, 1978 provides that an employer must give to his employees a written statement specifying certain particulars of the contract of employment.

However, cases come before the courts in which some of, but not all, the normal features of the relationship are present and the judge must decide whether the relationship exists in order to apply certain legal rules relating to employer and employee in making his judgment.

The Control Test

Salmond on the Law of Torts defines an employee (or servant) as 'any person employed by another to do work for him on the terms that he, the servant, is to be subject to the control and directions of his employer in respect of the manner in which his work is to be done'. The definition was approved by the court in *Hewitt* v. *Bonvin*, [1940] K.B. 188.

As we have seen, it is largely unnecessary in modern times to use the control test to establish the relationship of employer and employee. However, the control test is at the root of the distinction between *an employee* who works under a *contract of service* and an *independent contractor* who operates under *a contract for services*. For example, if Fred is employed as my chauffeur I would still have sufficient control over him to ask him to drive more slowly in a built-up area, but if he was a taxi-driver, many of whom are independent contractors, I would obviously not have, or even feel I had, the necessary control to insist on a change of speed.

In addition, the concept of control has been used by the courts *in situations where an employee is lent to another employer, or goes to work on the premises of another employer*. The control test may be applied where A lends his employee, B, to another person, C, so that C may be liable, under what is called the doctrine of vicarious liability, for damage caused by B to D even though there is admittedly no contract of service between C and B. There is, however, a presumption that control remains with A and A must prove that control has passed to C. The burden is a heavy one and the temporary employer will rarely be held liable, though it remains a possibility.

In addition to cases involving injuries to third parties, such as D, it should be noted that an employer also owes certain special duties to his employees, e.g. to provide safe equipment and premises and a safe system of working, and this may be a further reason for deciding whether C has become an employer by reason of the control test, as where, for example, the action is being brought by B against C in respect of injuries which B has suffered. Illustrations are provided by the following cases.

MERSEY DOCKS AND HARBOUR BOARD v. COGGINS AND GRIFFITHS (LIVERPOOL) LTD, [1946] 2 All E.R. 345 House of Lords

Facts

The Board owned and hired out mobile cranes driven by skilled operators who were engaged and paid by the Board. Coggins and Griffiths, who were stevedores, hired a crane and an operator, a Mr Newall, to unload a ship. The contract of hiring was subject to the Board's regulation 6, which said that the operator was to be the employee of the stevedores. In the course of unloading the ship a third party was injured as a result of the crane operator's negligence and the question arose whether the Board or Coggins and Griffiths were vicariously liable.

Judgment

It was held that the Board was vicariously liable for the operator's negligence.

Lord Macmillan said that it was always open to the general employer to say that his employee had been transferred but that the burden of proof lay with the general employer. He then went on to say 'I am of opinion that, on the facts of the present case, Newall was never so transferred from the service and control of the appellant Board to the service and control of the stevedores as to render the stevedores answerable for the manner in which he carried on his work of driving the crane. The stevedores were entitled to tell him where to go, what parcels to lift and where to take them, that is to say, they could direct him as to what they wanted him to do; but they had no authority to tell him how he was to handle the crane in doing his work.' Lord Macmillan also referred to the Board's regulation 6, and on this he said: 'But this does not mean that the appellant Board's drivers cease to be the servants of the appellant Board when they accompany cranes, which the appellant Board lets out on hire. Servants cannot be transferred from one service to another without their consent . . . .'

Comment

(i) The answers given by Mr Newall to counsel's questions in this case were highly important. At one point he said: 'I take no orders from anybody.' Commenting on this, Lord Simonds said that it was '. . . a sturdy answer which meant that he was a skilled man and knew his job and would carry it out in his own way. Yet ultimately he would decline to carry it out in the appellant's way at his peril, for in their hands lay the only sanction, the power of dismissal.'
(ii) On the matter of regulation 6 it was held in *Nokes* v. *Doncaster Amalgamated Collieries Ltd*, [1940] A.C. 1014 that a contract of service is a personal one and neither party can assign its obligations or rights to another.

GARRARD v. SOUTHEY, (A.E.) & CO. and STANDARD TELEPHONE & CABLES LTD, [1952] 1 All E.R. 597 High Court

Facts

Two persons employed by electrical contractors were sent to work in a factory on electrical installations. The electrical contractors continued to employ the men, paying their wages, making Social Security payments, and retaining the sole right to dismiss them. The electricians worked exclusively at the factory and used the factory canteen. The occupiers of the factory supplied them with all materials, tools and plant, except for certain special tools belonging to the electricians themselves. They were supervised by a foreman employed by the occupiers and they followed the system laid down in the factory. One of the electricians was injured when he fell from a defective trestle owned by some building contractors who were also working in the factory. The Court held that the occupiers of the factory, not the electrical contractors, owed the injured electrician the common law duty of an employer to his employee (to provide proper plant and equipment) and they were liable in damages to him for breach of that duty.

Comment

When this case was brought, the standard of care owed by an employer to an employee on his premises was higher than that owed to other persons or visitors on his premises. Since the Occupiers Liability Act, 1957 the duty to visitors has been raised, so that an occupier has a duty to take reasonable care in regard to visitors, whether they are employees or not: it is less important now to establish that the person injured was a temporary employee.

The Organisation or Integration Test

In earlier times the control test was a commonly used method of establishing the employer/employee relationship. The control test was basically satisfied if the employer could tell the employee WHAT to do and HOW to do it. In modern times this test is not realistic because many employers cannot tell their employees how to do their work. This might have caused difficulty in terms of making employers liable for injuries caused by skilled employees, such as surgeons.

However, this has not happened largely because of the organisation or integration test propounded by Lord Denning in *Stevenson, Jordan & Harrison Ltd* v. *Macdonald & Evans Ltd*. This case concerned copyright, and under copyright legislation the general position is that if an employee has 'in the course of his employment' produced a literary, musical, or artistic work which is capable of protection by copyright, then the first owner of that copyright is the employer. In order to arrive at a decision on this issue the Court of Appeal had first to consider which parts of the copyright in a book belonged to the author and which to this employer. If the author had prepared the material as an independent contractor the copyright was his. If, however, the material was prepared as part of his employment it belonged to his employer.

STEVENSON, JORDAN & HARRISON LTD v. MACDONALD & EVANS LTD, [1952] 1 TLR 101: Court of Appeal

Facts

An accountant and management consultant assigned to Macdonald

& Evans the copyright in a textbook on business management. Part of the book consisted of the text of a public lecture which he had given while employed by Stevenson, Jordan and another section contained material which he had compiled for the purpose of a management consultancy exercise he had conducted for Stevenson, Jordan.

Judgment
It was held by the Court of Appeal that the copyright in the lecture belonged to the accountant and he could therefore assign it to Macdonald & Evans because it was not delivered as part of his employment. However, Macdonald and Evans could be restrained from publishing the section of the book which was made up from the material compiled for the management consultancy exercise. This could be regarded as the property of Stevenson, Jordan.

'It is often easy to recognise a contract of service when you see it, but difficult to say wherein the difference lies. A ship's master, a chauffeur, and a reporter on the staff of a newspaper are all employed under a contract of service; but a ship's pilot, a taxi-man, and a newspaper contributor are employed under a contract for services. One feature which seems to run through the instances is that, under a contract of service, a man is employed as part of a business, and his work is done as an integral part of the business; whereas, under a contract for services, his work, although done for the business, is not integrated into it but is only accessory to it.' (per Lord Denning, L.J.)

The remarks of Lord Denning in *Roe* v. *Minister of Health*, [1954] 2 All E.R. 131, are also of interest in regard to the application of the organisation or integration principle. In the case negligence was alleged but not proved against a part-time consultant anaesthetist. Lord Denning said that if negligence had been proved the skilled nature of the anaesthetist's work would not have prevented his employer from being vicariously liable.

The use of the organisation test is not confined to cases involving skilled workers but has also been used to overcome some of the worst aspects of labour-only sub-contracting, as where a worker agrees to supply his services as an independent contractor. A main disadvantage to the worker is that he has no contract of employment and so the extensive duties of the employer, both at common law and by statute in terms of health, safety and welfare do not apply to the worker.

The following case shows, however, that the organisation test may be used to establish the relationship of employer and employee in a labour-only sub-contracting or 'lump' situation.

**FERGUSON v. JOHN DAWSON & PARTNERS (CONTRACTORS),
[1976] 3 All E.R. 817: Court of Appeal**

Facts

The plaintiff, who was working on the 'lump', was injured whilst working for the defendants, who were contractors. No deductions were made by the defendants for income tax or social security contributions and the plaintiff had been told that he was working 'purely as a lump labour force'. The defendants' site agent was responsible for hiring and dismissing the workmen, including the plaintiff; he told them what to do and moved them from site to site. If tools were required for the work, the defendants provided them. The plaintiff was injured when he fell off a roof which had no guard rail and he brought this action against the defendants on the basis that they were liable as his employers for failing to provide a guard rail on the flat roof which was required by construction regulations.

Judgment

The Court of Appeal held that whatever label was put on the parties' relationship, other factors should be considered, such as the fact that the defendants could dismiss the workmen, including the plaintiff, and tell them what to do and where to do it. Accordingly, the plaintiff was the employee of the defendants who were therefore liable under the construction regulations and must pay the plaintiff's damages for breach of that statutory duty.

VICARIOUS LIABILITY — GENERALLY

Because of the concept of vicarious liability an employer is liable for damage caused to another by his employee *while acting in the course of his employment*. This liability attaches to an employer even though he was not in any way at fault. This rule, which seems at first sight to be unfair to the employer, is based both upon *law* and *policy*.

So far as the law is concerned, employer and employee are regarded as *associated parties* in the business being carried out. If the business increases so that the employer cannot do it all with his own hands he must employ other hands and is in law responsible for the wrongs of those other hands as he would be for the wrongs of his own. This legal concept is expressed in the maxim *qui facit per alium facit per se* (he who does a thing through another does it himself).

The point of policy is designed to provide an injured person with a defendant who is likely to be able to pay any damages which the court may award if the action is successful. An employer generally profits from the employee's work and it is perhaps not entirely unreasonable that he should compensate those who are injured by the employee. Furthermore, the employer will normally insure against the risk and undoubtedly the cost of the insurance is respresented in the price at which he sells goods or services, so that in the end the injured party is compensated by those members of the public who buy those goods or services.

The Course of Employment — Generally

Whether an employee was or was not acting in the course of employment when he caused the injury for which it is sought to make his employer liable is a matter of *fact* not *law*, and we may, from time to time, disagree with a *fact* decision made by a judge in a particular case.

However, the following analysis of case law is illustrative of the way in which the courts have dealt with this important ingredient of employers' liability.

Acts extrinsic to the contract of service

BRITT v. GALMOYE & NEVILL, (1928) 44 TLR 294: High Court

Facts

Nevill was employed by Galmoye as a van driver. Nevill wanted to take a friend to the theatre after he had finished work and Galmoye lent Nevill his private motor car for this purpose. Nevill, by negligence, injured Britt and Britt's action against Galmoye was based upon vicarious liability so that it was necessary to deal with the issue of course of employment.

Judgment

It was held that as the journey was not on Galmoye's business and Galmoye was not in control, he was not liable for Nevill's act.

Comment

Britt's case is a rather obvious example of an act extrinsic to the contract of service. However, sometimes the court is called upon to make a more subtle decision. In particular it should be noted that an employee does not make his employer liable by doing some act which is of benefit to the employer during the course of what is basically an extrinsic activity. For example, in *Rayner* v. *Mitchell*, (1877) 2 CPD 257 a van man employed by a brewer took, without permission, a van from his employer's stables in order to deliver a child's coffin at the home of a relative. While he was returning the van to the stables he picked up some empty beer barrels and was afterwards involved in an accident which injured the plaintiff. The plaintiff sued the van man's employer and it was held that the employer was not liable. The journey itself was unauthorised and was not converted into an authorised journey merely because the employee performed some small act for the benefit of his employer during the course of it.

Wrongful and unauthorised methods of performing the contract of service

CENTURY INSURANCE CO. v. NORTHERN IRELAND ROAD TRANSPORT BOARD, [1942] AC 509: House of Lords

Facts

The driver of a petrol tanker was engaged in transferring petrol to an underground tank when he lit a cigarette and threw the match to the floor. This caused a fire and an explosion which did great damage, and the question of the liability of the Board, his employer, for that damage, arose.

Judgment

It was held that the employer was liable for the driver's negligence. His negligence was not independent of the contract of service but was a negligent way of discharging his duties under that contract of service.

Comment

(i) The case illustrates that it is no defence for an employer to show that the employee was performing in an improper way an act which was within the scope of his employment.

(ii) It is necessary here to consider situations in which an employee may be regarded as *impliedly* though not *expressly* authorised to do an act. An employee has an implied authority to do acts leading to the protection of his employer's property and the employer may be liable for damages caused by such acts even though they are somewhat excessive. For example, in *Poland* v. *John Parr & Sons*, [1927] 1 KB 236 a van driver, whilst off duty, was walking beside one of his employer's vans and saw a boy with his hand on a bag of sugar which was on the van. Thinking the boy was about to steal it he struck him and the boy fell and was run over and as a result lost his leg. It was held by the Court of Appeal that the employee's action was within his implied authority and the defendants, his employers, were liable in damages to the boy.

(iii) The court may as a matter of fact decide that the employee's act cannot be regarded as within his implied authority. This may be the case where the employee appears to have acted out of malice or personal vengeance. For example, in *Warren* v. *Henlys Ltd*, [1948] 2 All E.R. 935 the employer of a petrol pump attendant was not liable for the attendant's assault on a customer committed as a result of an argument over payment for petrol.

The point was also illustrated in *Daniels* v. *Whetstone Entertainments Ltd*, [1962] 2 Lloyd's Rep. 1 where the plaintiff was assaulted twice by a steward ejecting unruly persons from a dance hall. The first assault was made inside the dance hall and for this the steward's employer was liable. The second assault was made outside the hall and for this the steward's employer was not liable since the second assault appeared to be an act of personal retribution.

Acts expressly prohibited by employer

The fact that an employer has expressly forbidden his employee to do a particular act does not necessarily excuse him from vicarious liability in regard to damage caused by that act. There are two broad categories of case —

(a) Where the act itself is forbidden

RAND (JOSEPH) LTD v. CRAIG, [1919] 1 Ch. 1: Court of Appeal

Facts

The defendants employed carters to take rubbish from a site and deposit it on the defendants' dump. They were working on a bonus scheme related to the number of loads per day which they dumped. The defendants had strictly forbidden their employees to tip the rubbish elsewhere than on the authorised dump. However, some of the carters deposited their loads on the plaintiff's property which was nearer. The defendants were sued on the basis that they were vicariously liable in trespass, the plaintiffs arguing that the carters had general authority to cart and tip rubbish.

Judgment

It was held by the Court of Appeal that the defendant was not liable. The carters were employed to cart the rubbish from one definite place to another definite place. Shooting the rubbish on to the plaintiff's premises was a totally wrongful act not directly arising out of the duties they were employed to perform.

Comment

The point has also arisen in cases in which employees have given lifts to third parties in the employer's vehicle. In *Twine* v. *Bean's Express Ltd*, [1946] 1 All E.R. 202, a driver employed by the defendants gave a lift to a third person who was killed by reason of the employee's negligent driving. Instructions that employees were not to give lifts were displayed in the van. The Court held that the employers were not liable because in giving a lift to a third person the driver went beyond the scope of his employment and the passenger was a trespasser. In *Conway* v. *Geo. Wimpey & Co.*, [1951] 1 All E.R. 363, the facts were similar, although lifts were frequently given but this was unknown to the employers, and again they were not liable, the same line of argument being followed. The reasoning in these cases has been subjected to criticism because it is difficult to regard the plaintiff as a trespasser when the employee has invited him into the vehicle, and in both of the cases the employee did inflict injury on the passenger while in the course of his employment because in driving the vehicle he was clearly doing what he was employed to do.

However, it seems from the decision in *Young* v. *Edward Box & Co. Ltd*, [1951] 1 TLR 789 to be within the ostensible authority of a superior employee, and possibly of the driver, to sanction lifts for fellow employees but not strangers. That the matter is far from settled is illustrated by the following case.

ROSE v. PLENTY, [1976] 1 All E.R. 97: Court of Appeal

Facts

Leslie Rose, aged 13, was given to helping Mr Plenty, a milkman, to deliver milk. Co-operative Retail Services Ltd, who employed Mr Plenty, expressly forbade their milkmen to take boys on their floats or to get boys to help them deliver the milk. On one occasion while helping Mr Plenty, Leslie was sitting in the front of the float when his leg caught under the wheel. The accident was caused partly by Mr Plenty's negligence.

Judgment

It was held by the Court of Appeal (Lord Denning, M.R. and Scarman, L.J.) that Mr Plenty had been acting in the course of his employment so that his employers were liable to compensate Leslie Rose for his injuries. Lawton L.J. (dissenting) said that the cases of *Twine* and *Conway* were indistinguishable and that in giving Leslie a lift Mr Plenty had acted outside the scope of his employment.

Comment

There is really very little difference in the facts of *Rose* and *Twine* and *Conway* other than the fact that Leslie Rose was more than a mere hitch-hiker. His presence on the milk float was connnected with the delivery of the milk which was a reason connected with the employment and this is why Lord Denning and Scarman, L.J. felt able to distinguish *Twine* and *Conway*.

(b) **Where the prohibition relates only to the way in which an authorised act is carried out.**

LIMPUS v. LONDON GENERAL OMNIBUS CO., (1862) 1 H & C 526: Court of Common Pleas

Facts

The plaintiff's omnibus was overturned when the driver of the defendants' omnibus drove across it so as to be first at a bus stop to take all the passengers who were waiting. The defendants' driver admitted that the act was intentional, and arose out of bad feeling between the two drivers. The defendants had issued strict instructions to their drivers ·that they were not to obstruct other omnibuses.

Judgment

It was held by Willes, J. that the defendants were liable. Their driver was acting within the scope of his employment at the time of the collision, and it did not matter that the defendants had expressly forbidden him to act as he did.

Employee's fraudulent acts

In earlier times the court would not accept the principle of vicarious liability in fraud but gradually the concept was extended, first to cases in which the employee's fraud was committed for the employer's benefit, and later even to cases where the fraud was committed by the employee entirely for his own ends, as the following case illustrates.

LLOYD v. GRACE, SMITH & CO., [1912] AC 716: House of Lords

Facts

Smith was a Liverpool solicitor and Lloyd was a widow who owned two properties at Ellesmere Port and had also lent money on mortgage. She was not satisfied with the income from these investments and she went to see Smith's managing clerk, Sandles, for advice. He told her to sell the properties and call in the mortgages and re-invest the proceeds. At his request she signed two deeds which, unknown to her, transferred the properties and the mortgage to him. Sandles then mortgaged the properties and transferred the other mortgages for value and paid a private debt with the proceeds.

Judgment

It was held by the House of Lords that the firm of solicitors was liable. An employer could be vicariously liable for a tort committed by an employee entirely for his own ends.

Comment

This decision seems to contain an element of public policy and seems to be based on the principle that since someone must be the loser by reason of the deceit of the employee, it is more reasonable that the employer who engages and puts trust and confidence in the deceitful employee should be the loser rather than an outsider.

Employee's criminal acts

Criminal conduct on the part of an employee may be regarded as being in the course of his employment so that his employer will be liable at civil law for any loss or damage caused by the employee's criminal act.

MORRIS v. C. W. MARTIN & SONS LTD, [1965] 2 All E.R. 725: Court of Appeal

Facts

The plaintiff sent a mink stole to a furrier for the purpose of cleaning. With the plaintiff's consent the furrier gave it to the defendants to clean. While in the possession of the defendants the fur was stolen by a youth named Morrisey who had been employed by them for a few weeks only, though they had no grounds to suspect that he was dishonest. The plaintiff sued the defendants for conversion or negligence.

Judgment

The County Court judge held that the act of Morrisey, who had removed the stole by wrapping it round his body, was beyond the scope of his employment. The Court of Appeal held that the defendants were liable to the plaintiff because Morrisey had been entrusted with the stole in the course of his employment.

Comment

The above decision applies only in circumstances where the employee is entrusted with, or put in charge of, the goods by his employer. The mere fact that the employee's employment gives him the opportunity to steal the goods is not enough. 'A theft by any servant who is not employed to do anything in relation to the goods bailed is entirely outside the scope of his employment and cannot make the master liable. So in this case, if someone employed by the defendants in another depot had broken in and stolen the fur, the defendants would not have been liable. Similarly in my view if a clerk employed in the same depot had seized the opportunity of entering the room where the fur was kept and had stolen it, the defendants would not have been liable. . . . It might be otherwise if the master knew or ought to have known that his servant was dishonest, because then the master could be liable in negligence for employing him . . . .' (Per Salmon, L.J.) Presumably also if the employer's system of control is negligent so that non-entrusted employees are assisted in theft, the employer is also liable.

The Course of Employment — Corporations and *Ultra Vires*

Where the employer is a corporation there is a further complication in terms of its vicarious liability because the act of the employee may be beyond the corporation's powers, i.e. beyond the scope of what it is authorised to do by its constitution which may be a statute, as with the Coal Board, or a charter, as with a professional body, or the objects clause of the memorandum of association in the case of a registered company. We must therefore distinguish between *intra vires* acts and *ultra vires* acts by employees.

(a) *Intra vires* **activities**. Where an employee or agent of a corporation commits a tort while acting in the course of his employment in an *intra vires* activity, then the corporation is liable. Although it has been said that any tort committed on behalf of a corporation must be *ultra vires* (since Parliament does not authorise corporations to commit torts) this view is fallacious, since the corporation can have legal liability without legal capacity. A corporation is liable, therefore, under the principles of vicarious liability for the torts of its employees or agents committed on *intra vires* activities.

(b) *Ultra vires* **activities.** As regards *ultra vires* acts, a corporation will not be liable if an employee or agent engages in an *ultra vires* activity *without express authority*. Thus in *Poulton* v. *London & South Western Railway Co.*, (1867) L.R. 2 QB 534 the plaintiff was arrested by a station-master for non-payment of carriage in respect of his horse. The defendants, who were the ·employers of the station master, had power to detain passengers for non-payment cf their own fare, but for no other reason. The Court held that since there was no express authorisation of the arrest by the defendants, the station-master was acting outside the scope of his employment and the defendants were not liable for the wrongful arrest.

On the other hand, where a tortious act is *ultra vires* but has been *expressly authorised*, the corporation is liable for it. Thus in *Campbell* v. *Paddington Borough Council*, [1911] 1 KB 869 the members of the council, in accordance with a resolution duly passed, authorised the erection of a stand in Burwood Place in order that members of the council might view the funeral procession of King Edward VII passing along the Edgware Road. The plaintiff, who occupied certain premises in Burwood Place, often let the premises for the purpose of viewing public processions passing along the Edgware Road. The stand obstructed the view of the funeral procession from the plaintiff's house and she was unable to let the premises for that purpose. The Court held that as the stand constituted a public nuisance the plaintiff could maintain an action for the special damage which she had sustained through the loss of view. The corporation were properly sued, and the fact that the erection of the stand was probably *ultra vires*, there being no specific power in its charter to erect one, did not matter.

Vicarious Liability — Employer's Defences

If the employee's negligence is established there are three main defences which an employer can raise in an action against him for vicarious liability for that negligence. These are set out below.

An exclusion clause in a contract or notice

Under s. 2(1) of the Unfair Contract Terms Act, 1977 an employer, like other people, cannot by reference to any contract term or notice given to persons generally, or to particular persons, *exclude* or *restrict* his liability for death or bodily injury resulting from his own negligence or that of his employee.

As regards other types of damage, e.g. damage to property, the exempting clause or notice is valid if, and only if, it satisfies the test of reasonableness.

Thus, in the case of a dry cleaning contract, if by the negligence of employees cleaning material is not properly removed so that the owner of the clothing contracts a skin disease, to which he is not especially susceptible, no exclusion clause in the contract for cleaning or in a notice in the shop can remove or restrict the employer's liability for this bodily harm.

However, if the clothing is, by reason of an employee's negligence, merely damaged and there is no resulting physical injury, then an exclusion clause or notice might operate to remove or restrict the liability of the employer if the judge thinks it reasonable for it to do so in the circumstances.

The test of reasonableness has yet to be worked out by the courts, but it is generally true to say that the device of an exclusion clause in a contract or notice has lost most of its force as an employer's defence.

It should also be noted that knowledge of the excluding contractual term or notice does not operate as assumption of risk (see below).

Assumption of risk

This is alternatively called the defence of *volenti non fit injuria* (to one who is willing no harm is done). There are two main aspects of this defence, i.e. deliberate harm and accidental harm.

In the first case the plaintiff's assent may prevent his complaining of some deliberate conduct of the defendant which would normally be actionable. Thus if A takes part in a game of Rugby football he must be presumed to accept the rough tactics which are a characteristic and *normal* part of the game, and any damage caused would not give rise to a successful action, although if the same tactics were employed in the street, a successful action could be sustained. Similarly, although to stick a knife into a person would normally be actionable, if a surgeon does it with the consent of the patient it is not so.

A different situation arises in what are known as the *rescue cases*. In these the plaintiff is injured while intervening to save life or property put in danger by the defendant's negligence. If the intervention is a reasonable thing to do for the saving of life or property, then this does not constitute assumption of risk, nor does the defence of contributory negligence (see below) apply.

HAYNES v. HARWOOD & SON, [1935] 1 KB 146: Court of Appeal

Facts

The defendants' employee left his van unattended in a street and the horses bolted with it. The plaintiff was a police constable on duty in a police station and seeing the horses bolting into a crowded street and realising that, unless the horses were stopped, people in the street, including many children, would be likely to be injured, he darted out of the police station, and, at great risk to himself, seized one of the horses and managed to bring both to a standstill. He was injured in doing so and sued the defendants in negligence.

Judgment

The Court of Appeal held that the defendants were liable and that the plaintiff was not guilty of contributory negligence. Furthermore, the damage was not too remote. The defendants also alleged assumption of risk by the plaintiff, but the Court decided that the plaintiff's knowledge of the risk was not a bar to his claim in this situation.

However, if the intervention is not reasonable then the defences of *volenti* and contributory negligence may apply.

CUTLER v. UNITED DAIRIES (LONDON) LTD, [1933] 2 KB 297

Facts

The defendants' carman left the defendants' horse and van, two wheels only being properly chained, while he delivered milk. The horse, being startled by the noise coming from a river steamer, bolted down the road and into a meadow. It stopped in the meadow and was followed there by the carman who, being in an excited state, began to shout for help. The plaintiff, a spectator, went to the carman's assistance and tried to hold the horse's head. The horse lunged and the plaintiff was injured. The plaintiff sued the defendants alleging negligent control by their employee of the horse and van.

Judgment

The Court held that in the circumstances the plaintiff voluntarily and freely assumed the risk. This was not an attempt to stop a runaway horse so that there was no sense of urgency to impel the plaintiff. He therefore knew of the risk and had had time to consider it, and by implication must have agreed to incur it.

A person may take greater risk in protecting or rescuing life than in the mere protection of property, though even in protecting property reasonable risk may be taken.

HYETT v. GREAT WESTERN RAILWAY CO., [1948] 1 KB 345

Facts

The plaintiff was employed by a firm of wagon-repairers and he was on the defendants' premises with their authority to carry out his duties. While repairing a wagon he saw smoke rising from one of the defendants' wagons in the same siding and went to investigate. The floor of the wagon, which contained paraffin oil, was in flames. The plaintiff was trying to get the drums of paraffin oil out when one of them exploded and injured him. Evidence showed that the defendants knew that there was a paraffin leakage in the wagon, but had nevertheless allowed it to remain in the siding. The plaintiff now sued the defendants for damages in negligence.

Judgment

The Court held that the plaintiff was entitled to recover damages from the defendants, and that the maxim *volenti non fit injuria* did not apply. A person may take reasonable risks in trying to preserve property put in danger by another's negligence.

The defence of assumption of risk or consent has most often been raised in an employment law context when employees have sued their employers for injuries received at work, and we shall consider these cases in Chapter 6. However, the defence is available to an employer when a claim is based on vicarious liability for an employee's negligence is made against him, as *Cutler* and *Haynes* show.

Contributory negligence

Sometimes when an accident occurs both parties have been negligent, and this raises the defence of contributory negligence. At one time a plaintiff guilty of contributory negligence could not recover any damages unless the defendant could, with reasonable care, have avoided the consequences of the plaintiff's contributory want of care. Thus the courts were often concerned to find out who had the last chance of avoiding the accident, and this led to some unsatisfactory decisions.

Now, however, under the Law Reform (Contributory Negligence) Act, 1945, liability is apportionable between plaintiff and defendant. The claim is not defeated but damages may be reduced according to the degree of the fault of the plaintiff.

It should be mentioned that a young child will seldom, if ever, be guilty of contributory negligence and the contributory negligence of an adult who happens to be with the child is no defence to an action brought by the child.

Again, the defence in the context of employment law has most often been used where an employee is suing his employer for injuries received at work and the employer alleges that the employee was to some extent to blame so that the employee's damages should be reduced. These cases will be considered in Chapter 6.

However, an employer who was sued as vicariously liable for the tort of an employee could, if the circumstances were right, allege that the third party's damages should be reduced on the grounds of the third party's contributory negligence.

It should also be noted that the employer is vicarious responsible for the contributory negligence of his employees in the course of their employment. Thus, if A employs B as a lorry driver, and B is involved in an accident with C, which causes damage to the lorry, then if A sues C for this damage, the amount of money A will receive may be reduced by an appropriate percentage representing the contributory negligence, if any, of B.

Vicarious Liability — Indemnity or Contribution from Employee

Indemnity

In the vicarious liability situation where the employee has been negligent and the employer has not, both are nevertheless regarded as joint tortfeasors and although the employer will normally pay the damages following a successful action, he has a right to claim an *indemnity*, i.e. the whole amount he has paid out, from the negligent employee, because it is a term implied by common law that an employee will indemnify his employer for loss caused to the employer by the employee.

LISTER v. ROMFORD ICE & COLD STORAGE CO. LTD, [1957] 1 All E.R. 125: House of Lords

Facts

The defendants' lorry driver negligently reversed the company's vehicle into another employee of the company (his father) who received damages from the company under the doctrine of vicarious liability. The defendants were insured against this liability and the insurance company paid the damages and, under the doctrine of subrogation, sued the lorry driver in the name of the company to recover what they had paid.

Judgment

It was unanimously held by the House of Lords that the lorry driver, as an employee of the company, owed them a duty to perform his work with reasonable care and skill, and that an employee who involves his employer in vicarious liability by reason of negligence is liable in damages to the employer for breach of contract. This liability arises out of an implied term in the contract of service to indemnify the employer for loss caused to him by the employee's negligence. The damages will in such a case amount to a complete indemnity in respect of the amount which the employer has been held vicariously liable to pay the injured plaintiff.

Comment

It should be noted that employers are not likely in ordinary circumstances to be required by their insurers to bring an action to enforce their right to an indemnity, which was the position in *Lister's* case. A committee was set up to deal with the implications of the *Lister* case. As an outcome of its report all members of the British Insurance Association entered into an agreement to the effect that they would not enforce their rights of subrogation in an employer's liability policy, except where there was evidence of collusion or wilful misconduct on the part of the employee. A number of other insurance organisations have also entered into similar agreements. Thus actions against employees for indemnities, either by the employer's insurance company or by the employer himself, are likely to be rare since, amongst other things, such actions are not popular with trade unions.

Contribution

If, for example, the employer has been negligent himself and so contributed to the damage, the employer will recover only a contribution and not an indemnity from the employee under the provisions of the Law Reform (Married Women and Tortfeasors) Act, 1935. Thus the employer will not receive all that he has paid to the third party but only that proportion attributable to the employee's negligence.

JONES v. MANCHESTER CORPORATION, [1952] 2 QB 852: Court of Appeal

Facts

A patient in a hospital died under anaesthetic. The doctor who administered the anaesthetic was negligent as were his employers, the hospital board, because they should not have allowed him to administer that particular anaesthetic as they knew that he had only a slight experience of it. The plaintiff, who was the widow of the patient, obtained a judgment against the board and the doctor for damages. The board and the doctor then claimed an indemnity from each other for any damages and costs that they might be asked to pay.

Judgment

The Court of Appeal held that the board was not entitled to an indemnity against the doctor but apportioned responsibility as 20% to the doctor and 80% to the hospital board, thus allowing the hospital board to recover 20% of what it had paid to the plaintiff from the doctor.

2 Contract of Employment—Generally

FORMATION — GENERALLY

The ordinary principles of the law of contract apply, so that in a contract of employment there must be an offer and acceptance, which is in effect the agreement. There must be an intention to create legal relations, consideration and capacity, together with genuineness of consent by the parties to the terms of the contract. In addition, the contract must not be contrary to public policy.

However, it is not intended to go into the detail of the general law of contract but only to highlight certain matters which are of importance in the context of employment law.

Contract of Adhesion

In many cases the contract of employment cannot be regarded as a separate *bargain* between employer and employee. The terms of the contract are often fixed by *collective agreements* made between one or more trades unions and one or more employers or employers' associations, or are governed by *statutory regulations* operated, for example, by Wages Councils who fix minimum wages and other terms and conditions of employment in certain industries.

Thus since the terms are often not negotiated by the parties, the contract may be regarded as a contract of adhesion, i.e. one to which both parties must adhere and cannot bargain their way out of.

Parties to the Contract

It is necessary to consider here certain categories of persons whose legal position is unusual in terms of the making of a contract of employment.

Minors

These are persons under 18 years of age who do not have a full contractual capacity. Our concern is only with those aspects of the law which relate to minors in the context of ordinary contracts of employment and apprentice-ship.

Ordinary contracts of employment

A minor is bound by beneficial contracts, and since it is obviously beneficial for a minor to obtain a livelihood, an ordinary contract of employment is binding on the minor. However, this is not so where the terms of the contract are onerous, although the court will look at the whole contract and not merely at isolated terms, arriving at a decision on the *total* effect of the agreement. The two cases which follow provide an interesting contrast.

DE FRANCESCO v. BARNUM, (1890) 45 Ch.D. 430: Court of Appeal

Facts

Two minors bound themselves in contract to the plaintiff for seven years to be taught stage dancing. The minors agreed that they would not accept any engagements without his consent. They later accepted an engagement with Barnum and the plaintiff sued Barnum for interfering with the contractual relationship between himself and the minors, and also to enforce the apprenticeship deed against the minors and to obtain damages for its breach. The contract was, of course, for the minors' benefit and was *prima facie* binding on them. However, when the Court considered the deed in greater detail it emerged that there were certain onerous terms in it. For example, the minors bound themselves not to marry during the apprenticeship; the payment was hardly generous, the plaintiff agreeing to pay them 9*d*. (approx. 4½*p*) per night and 6*d*. (2½*p*) for matinee appearances for the first three years, and 1*s*. (5*p*) per night and 6*d*. (2½*p*) for matinee performances during the remainder of the apprenticeship. The plaintiff did not undertake to maintain them whilst they were unemployed and did not undertake to find them engagements. The minors could also be engaged in performances abroad at a fee of 5*s*. (25*p*) per week. Further, the plaintiff could terminate the contract if he felt that the minors were not suitable for the career of dancer. It appeared from the contract that the minors were at the absolute disposal of the plaintiff.

Judgment

It was held by the Court of Appeal that the deed was an unreasonable one and was therefore unenforceable against the minors. Barnum could not, therefore, be held liable, since the tort of interference with a contractual relationship presupposes the existence of an enforceable contract.

CLEMENTS v. LONDON & NORTH WESTERN RAILWAY, [1894] 2 QB 482: Court of Appeal

Facts

Clements became a porter with the railway company and agreed to join the company's insurance scheme and to forgo his rights under the Employers' Liability Act, 1880. He sustained an injury at work and claimed under the company's scheme. He then made a claim under the Act on the grounds that the contract was not for his benefit since it deprived him of an action under the Act. The company's scheme was on the whole a favourable one because it covered more injuries than the statute but the scale of compensation was lower.

Judgment

It was held by the Court of Appeal that the contract as a whole was for Clements' benefit, although he was a minor, and was therefore binding on him. Thus he had no claim under the Act.

Contracts of apprenticeship

A contract of apprenticeship must satisfy the rules relating to beneficial contracts. The contract is, of course, within the beneficial class and will be binding provided its terms are not onerous (see *De Francesco* v. *Barnum*, above).

A contract of apprenticeship must be in writing, otherwise it operates as a mere contract of employment.

KIRKBY v. TAYLOR, [1910] 1 KB 529: Divisional Court of the King's Bench Division

Facts

Taylor had served an apprenticeship with his father, who was a registered chemist. The contract of apprenticeship was not in writing. When his apprenticeship had finished Kirkby, who was a Customs and Excise officer, laid an information before magistrates alleging that Taylor had committed an offence under the Medicines Stamp Act, 1812 by selling certain drugs without having served a regular apprenticeship, as the Act required. The magistrates felt that a regular apprenticeship could be served under an oral contract but they sent the case to the Divisional Court of the King's Bench Division for further consideration.

Judgment

It was held by the Divisional Court that Taylor had not served a regular apprenticeship because the contract with his father had not been in writing. The Court based its decision on the provisions of the Apprentices Act, 1814 which allows apprenticeship agreements to be in writing, whereas earlier legislation of Elizabethan times had required apprenticeship agreements to be under seal. The Divisional Court remitted the case to the magistrates to convict Taylor.

A contract of apprenticeship is technically not a contract of service but is treated as such for the purposes of employment legislation including the statutory provisions relating to unfair dismissal and redundancy. The difference between a contract of apprenticeship and a contract of employment can best be illustrated by examining the law relating to the termination of the apprenticeship contract.

Termination during period of training

(a) **At common law.** So far as the common law is concerned, behaviour justifying dismissal of an ordinary employee will not necessarily justify dismissal of an apprentice.

DUNK v. WALLER (GEORGE) & SON, [1970] 2 All E.R. 630: Court of Appeal

Facts

Dunk was apprenticed in December 1964 to Waller under an agreement with an express clause entitling his employers to terminate it if the apprentice was guilty of misconduct. Dunk passed his first engineering examination at the second attempt, but although his general standard of work was average, reports on his prospects of passing the second examination were unfavourable. His employers, on receiving a report from the local technical college to this effect, wrote him a letter telling him that they had no alternative but to terminate the apprenticeship. Dunk said that he had no intention of terminating the agreement. The company wrote offering him factory work, which he declined. Instead he obtained unemployment pay for 57 weeks of the 15 months' unexpired period of his apprenticeship and worked as a labourer in a factory for a further eight weeks at £20 per week. Dunk therefore brought an action claiming damages against his employers for breach of contract.

Judgment

In the Court of Appeal Lord Denning, M.R. said that the letter terminating the agreement was a breach of the contract which the employers had no right to terminate, for Dunk had not been guilty of misconduct and the agreement should have run for the whole four years. An apprentice got much less than he would earn in the open market. By the termination of the agreement he was deprived of other benefits such as training, instruction, experience, and of a certificate at the end to show that he had served his full period. Dunk was therefore entitled to damages for the loss of earnings, during the part which remained of the term; also for his loss of future prospects of getting a better post and wages because of his training and experience. On the basis that Dunk had lost £10 a week, which was his weekly wage for the 57 weeks during which he was unemployed, he was entitled to £570, less £270 received as unemployment pay, a round sum of £300 for the short-term loss.

Regarding the long-term loss, the evidence was that Dunk would have been able to start at £1 or £2 a week more if he had served an apprenticeship. For this he was given a further £80, plus £20 for the expense of finding other work, a total of £500.

Comment

Considering this case as it affects solicitors' and accountants' articled clerks, it seems that, like everyone else suffering from a breach of contract, the articled clerk would have an obligation to mitigate his damage which would mean seeking other articles. If these were available, the loss of earnings, other than during articles, would presumably be simply for the period for which his admission as a solicitor or accountant was delayed because of a break in the articles. If, on the other hand, because of the difficulty some people have in obtaining articles, he never became re-articled, the possible liability could be very great.

(b) **By statute.** The attitude of industrial tribunals applying statute law is much the same as that of the ordinary courts of law, and dismissals during the period of apprenticeship are usually, but not inevitably, regarded as unfair. Thus in *Paviour & Thomas* v. *Whittons Transport (Cullompton)*, [1975] I.R.L.R. 258 a receiver gave notice to a number of employees, including two apprentices, to reduce staff, no arrangements having been made with another firm to take over the apprentices. This dismissal of the apprentices was held to be unfair although redundancy can justify dismissal of ordinary employees. However, a contrast is provided by *Townrow* v. *Phillip Davies*,

(1977) 121 S.J. 354. In this case the defendant, a solicitor, employed the plaintiff as an articled clerk. The defendant was a sole principal and was forced by ill-health to amalgamate his practice with that of another firm. That firm was not willing to agree to the plaintiff continuing his articles with the defendant or with any other partner in the firm. The defendant tried to find alternative articles for the plaintiff but did not succeed. The plaintiff then complained that he had been unfairly dismissed by the defendant. It was held by the Employment Appeal Tribunal that the defendant had in all the circumstances acted reasonably and the plaintiff's complaint of unfair dismissal could not be sustained. Again in *Finch* v. *Betabake (Anglia)*, [1977] I.R.L.R. 470 the plaintiff, an apprentice motor mechanic, was dismissed by the defendants after they had received a medical report confirming that as a result of defective eyesight he could not be employed as a motor mechanic apprentice without undue danger to himself or other employees. The plaintiff claimed unfair dismissal, but it was held by the Employment Appeal Tribunal that in the circumstances of the case the dismissal was fair.

Termination after expiry of period of training. Here we are concerned with the situation in which the contract of apprenticeship has expired but the employer does not wish to continue to employ the former apprentice. There would seem to be three possible situations here so far as statute law is concerned:

(i) A contract of apprenticeship is invariably for a fixed term of more than two years, and although failure to renew a fixed term contract is under s 55(2) (b) of the Employment Protection (Consolidation) Act, 1978 a dismissal, the apprentice may under s 142 *ibid.* agree in writing under the contract to waive his rights to a claim for unfair dismissal or redundancy. This should prevent such claims provided the apprentice was aware of the effect of his waiver so that his consent was real. Otherwise the waiver might be ineffective.

(ii) There may be substantial reasons for refusing to continue the employment. Thus in *Small* v. *Lex Mead Southampton*, [1977] I.R.L.R. 48 the plaintiff was employed as a mechanic under an apprenticeship for four years. He received oral and written warnings after there had been complaints about his work during the period June 1974 to June 1976. He was dismissed in June 1976 having completed his apprenticeship in May of the same year after he had repaired a car which afterwards caught fire when being driven. An industrial tribunal held that he had been dismissed because his fixed term contract of apprenticeship had expired without being renewed. However, there were substantial reasons for dismissal, so that the plaintiff's claim for unfair dismissal failed.

(iii) It may be that the expiry of a fixed term contract of apprenticeship does not give rise to a claim for unfair dismissal since it is a fixed term contract which would not be renewed in the sense of an engagement for another term as an apprentice. This was the view of the industrial tribunal in *Small* v. *Lex Mead Southampton* (above).

Apprenticeship — the role of the training boards and professional bodies

A recent development in the field of apprenticeship is the supervisory role played by joint industry training boards who are commonly parties to the apprenticeship contract within industry. In addition, the boards regulate the number and quality of apprenticeships within an industry and finance training by levy.

They have more than a supervisory role and can terminate apprenticeships where training is inadequate, arrange continuation with another employer and act as arbitrator in disputes. Under arrangements with the boards the current industrial contract also provides that an apprentice cannot be made redundant unless the employer finds an alternative apprenticeship and pays full wages in the meantime. In addition, the JIB must be informed of an intended dismissal and can determine its validity. Decisions of tribunals of this kind are potentially liable to review by the courts but, because the machinery is adequate, recourse to the courts is rare.

Those who are not covered by JIBs, such as solicitors' and accountants' articled clerks, are in a weaker position; the professional bodies concerned have only limited powers to supervise and check training, nor do they find it easy to enforce minimum conditions of employment, and in terms of finance there is no levy system. These problems might be overcome if the institutes concerned were to set up a body similar to joint industry training boards. Solutions are of pressing importance, not only in terms of domestic law, but also in terms of the European Social Charter which will guide UK legislation in the future and which, amongst other things, requires fair and effective training arrangements and the adequate protection of young workers generally.

Directors

Directors may be fee-paid supervisors acting in some ways as trustees for the shareholders, or senior executives or managers who work whole-time as directors of the company and who sometimes combine this with the giving of a professional service to the company, for example, as an accountant.

All directors may be removed by the members by ordinary resolution in general meeting under s 184 of the Companies Act, 1948 and it is not necessary to allege any form of misconduct against them. Removal under s 184 *ibid.* does not prevent the director removed from bringing an action for damages for wrongful dismissal, if, but only if, he has a service contract, *express* or *implied*, with the company which entitles him to a period of notice which the company has not given or is for a term of years which has not expired.

To explain an implied contract let us suppose that A is appointed director for life by the articles of Boxo Limited on its formation. The articles are not a contract between the company and its directors (*Beattie* v. *Beattie Limited*, [1938] 3 All E.R. 214), but if A works as a director on the basis of the articles there is an implied contract on the terms of the articles (*Re New British Iron*, *ex parte Beckwith*, [1898] 1 Ch. 324). Thus if A was removed under s 184 of the 1948 Act after serving, say, five years, he would have a claim for damages for wrongful dismissal in the ordinary courts of law.

As regards claims for unfair dismissal and redundancy before industrial tribunals, directors who are employed under express service contracts will normally be engaged for a fixed term of two years or more and may have been required in the contract to waive the right to claim for unfair dismissal or redundancy if the contract is not renewed, as s 142 of the Employment Protection (Consolidation) Act, 1978 allows. Directors working under implied contracts will not normally have waived these rights.

However, a director who is an employee and who is removed before his contractual term, express or implied, expires has a claim before an industrial tribunal for unfair dismissal or redundancy, and this may be a quicker procedure than a court action for wrongful dismissal, though much depends upon salary as there is a ceiling placed on awards for unfair dismissal (see p. 96).

Such claims are only available to employee directors, i.e. persons who, under s 153 of the Employment Protection (Consolidation) Act, 1978, work under a contract of service, written or oral, express or implied.

PARSONS v. ALBERT J. PARSONS & SONS LTD, *The Times*, 14 November 1978: Court of Appeal

Facts

Mr Albert Parsons was the founder of a family haulage business. He died leaving three sons and a company was formed to carry on the business. Later on subsidiary companies were set up to sell and hire motor vehicles, and the applicant in this case, Mr Leonard Parsons, spent a considerable amount of his time with the subsidiary companies while his mother and two brothers were more concerned with the main business. The two elder brothers, Leonard and Kenneth, were made directors for life in the main company and all three brothers worked in the business but no fee or salary or contract of service was agreed or drawn up. At the end of each year directors' emoluments were voted and over a period of some ten years the average emolument of each of the brothers was some £10,000 p.a. In 1976 differences between the brothers arose, and at an extraordinary general meeting Leonard was removed from his executive duties, this including the signing of cheques. At a later extraordinary general meeting he was removed from his position as director. He then claimed compensation for unfair dismissal and the matter of whether or not he was entitled even to apply turned on whether he was an employee within the definition in s 153 of the Employment Protection (Consolidation) Act, 1978.

Judgment

In considering the matter Lord Denning referred in particular to the company's accounts which had been prepared by an experienced accountant. The accounts showed:

(a) that no item of wages or salary for the brothers was shown although they were for other employees;

(b) that for national insurance purposes the brothers were put in as self-employed;

(c) that in general terms the accounts as presented put the view that the brothers were full-time directors being remunerated by way of directors' fees.

A further point which was regarded as important by Lord Denning was that although s 26 of the Companies Act, 1967 required the company to keep copies of directors' service contracts or a memorandum thereof for inspection by members, there was no such contract or memorandum thereof in the company's files in respect of its directors. In view of these circumstances Leonard Parsons was not an employee and so not entitled to apply for compensation for unfair dismissal.

Managing director

Usually an arrangement by which day-to-day management is left in the hands of the full-time or executive directors is given formal effect by the full-time directors, or one or more of them being appointed managing director or directors and being given powers of management which are exercisable without reference to the board.

Before such an appointment can be made the articles of the company must so provide. Table A, Art. 107 of the Companies Act, 1948 provides for the appointment of a managing director (or directors) by the board and not by the shareholders and further states that he shall not be subject to retirement by rotation. Generally, one-third of a board retires each year and they are eligible for re-election at a general meeting of members. However, under Art. 107 a person ceases to be a managing director if for any other reason he ceases to be a director, as where he is removed, though where a managing director has a service contract, express or implied, the company will be liable in damages for breach of that contract. Art. 108 allows the directors to fix the remuneration of the managing director and it will be seen that where a company's articles are in the form of Table A, the managing director is largely independent of the shareholders, though not of the board.

Partners

An existing partner cannot be employed by the firm. The firm is not a *persona* at law as a company is and so a partner can only enter into a contract of service with himself and other partners as *joint employers*, which is not possible at law. A former partner could, of course, be employed by the remaining partners.

The partners may, of course, be paid a salary as a way of dividing profits, particularly where one partner does more work in the firm than others, so that to pay him a salary before profits are divided boosts his share of income from the firm. However, this does not mean that he is an employee.

The position of partners who are wholly remunerated by salary — salaried partners, as they are known — is unclear, but the following case gives some indication of judicial thinking.

STEKEL v. ELLICE, [1973] 1 All E.R. 465: Chancery Division

Facts

Ellice, a chartered accountant and sole partner, took in Stekel as a salaried partner under an agreement for a fixed remuneration. Ellice provided the capital and took all the profits. No steps were taken towards a full partnership agreement and in 1970 the salaried arrangement was dissolved by mutual consent. However, the business continued exactly as before, Stekel receiving only his salary. In this action Stekel claimed that on the termination of the salaried arrangement there was a new partnership at will and under s 24 of the Partnership Act, 1890 he was entitled from that time to share profits equally with Ellice. He therefore asked for an order dissolving the firm and for accounts at the date of dissolution to ascertain his share in the firm. The defendant relied upon the provisions of s 27 of the Partnership Act, 1890 which states that when a fixed-term partnership has expired but the partners carry on in business they do so on terms and conditions similar to those prevailing whilst the fixed-term contract was in existence, so that Stekel was only entitled to his salary even after the original salaried arrangement was brought to an end.

Judgment

Megarry, J. preferred the defendant's argument, and although that meant that Stekel was a partner in the firm, it was not the case that every partner had a right to ask for an order dissolving it. The judge found as a fact that Stekel had no proprietary interest in the firm, either in its capital, goodwill, or its clients, and for that reason could not have an order for dissolution. It followed from that, of course, that Stekel would not benefit by any order for accounts and this was also denied him.

Comment

There was no full argument before the judge on the position of salaried partners generally; he did say *obiter* that he thought the majority of salaried partners had no claim to an order for the dissolution of the firm on the ground that in general terms they would have no capital interest in it. This makes the position of a salaried partner rather difficult because it is generally believed that a salaried partner is liable for the debts of the firm to third parties. It may be that the court would grant an order of dissolution to a salaried partner where a partnership was making a loss because it would only be in this way that he could cut down his liability to third parties for the firm's debts. Furthermore, an order for dissolution might be granted to a salaried partner who had a long fixed-term contract at a salary which became unreasonably low as a result of inflation on the ground that a dissolution order in such a case would be just and equitable under s 35 of the Act of 1890.

Agents

An agent is a person who is engaged to make contracts on behalf of another person who is called the principal. It does not follow, however, that the relationship is that of employer and employee and the facts of each case must be examined carefully by the courts.

However, an agent who merely receives commission in respect of contracts which he successfully negotiates, e.g. an estate agent, is not an employee and has none of the special rights in terms, for example, of a claim for unfair dismissal or redundancy which employment law confers on employees properly so called.

However, some persons have a dual role as employees and agents. For example, an usherette in a theatre is an employee when she shows patrons to their seats and an agent if she sells them a programme. Such a person would, of course, have employee rights in terms, for example, of a claim for unfair dismissal or redundancy.

Immigrants

As regards immigrant employees, there is no difficulty in respect of the making of a contract of service since they have no disability at law unless they are enemy aliens, when the contract is void.

However, of more importance is the effect of the Immigration Act, 1971 and other relevant legislation. This can be summarised in terms of the seven categories of persons who might be seeking employment in the UK. These categories and their legal powers in terms of entry for work are set out below.

(a) **United Kingdom citizens.** These are, for example, people who were born in the UK. They are free to re-enter the UK and can move freely within the EEC. They can take UK jobs without a work permit and cannot be deported.

(b) **Patrial Commonwealth citizens,** e.g. Canadians, Australians and New Zealanders with a UK-born parent. They can enter the UK but cannot move freely within the EEC. They can take UK jobs without a permit and cannot be deported.

(c) **Non-patrial Commonwealth citizens.** These are Commonwealth citizens with a UK grandparent. They are, in the main, UK-descended Australians, Canadians and New Zealanders. They can only enter the UK on production of entry clearance which is freely given by the immigration authorities. They cannot move freely within the EEC but can take UK jobs without a permit. They can be deported.

(d) **Citizens of the Irish Republic.** They can enter the UK and move freely within the EEC. They can also take UK jobs without a work permit. They can be deported.

(e) **Non-patrials who are EEC nationals.** These are citizens of EEC countries, such as France and Holland. They have no right under UK law to enter and stay in the UK because they are not patrials. However, in this connection the following case is instructive.

VAN DUYN v THE HOME OFFICE, [1974] 3 All E.R. 178: Chancery Division

Facts

Yvonne van Duyn, a Dutch national, was a Scientologist who tried to enter the United Kingdom on 9 May 1973. She was refused entry on the grounds that the Secretary of State considered it undesirable to give anyone leave to enter the United Kingdom on the basis of, or in the employment of, the Church of Scientology because its activities were considered contrary to public policy. Miss van Duyn did not appeal under the Immigration Act of 1971 but sought a declaration in the Chancery Division that she was entitled to enter the country. She claimed that Art. 48 of the Treaty of Rome, which allowed nationals of member states of the EEC to accept offers of employment and to remain in a member state for the purposes of employment, applied in her case. She conceded that these rights were subject to 'limitation justified on grounds of public policy, public security or public health' (Art. 48(3)), but said that Art. 3 of Directive 64/221 of 25 February 1964, provided that measures taken on grounds of public policy should be based exclusively on the personal conduct of the individual concerned and not merely on the basis of employment by a given organisation.

Judgments

In the Chancery Division the Vice Chancellor (Sir John Pennycuick) made the first reference to the European Court (i.e. the Court of Justice of the European Communities) under the Rules of the Supreme Court Order 114. Among the matters referred was the question whether or not the directive of 1964 was 'directly applicable so as to confer on individuals rights enforceable by them in the Courts of the United Kingdom'. The Court of Justice decided ([1975] 3 All E.R. 190):

(i) That obligations imposed on member states by Art. 48(1) and (2) of the Treaty to abolish discrimination based on nationality as regards employment were directly applicable so as to confer on individuals rights enforceable by them in the courts of member states, since those provisions imposed on member states precise obligations which did not require the adoption of any further measures by the Community or member states;

(ii) That although Art. 189 of the Treaty provided that regulations were to 'be directly applicable' in member states, it did not follow that Directives could not be applicable also. In order to determine whether a Directive was directly applicable it was necessary to examine whether the nature, general scheme and wording of the provision were capable of having a direct effect on the relations between member states and individuals. On that basis Art. 3(1) of Directive 64/221 was directly applicable since it laid down an obligation which was not subject to any exception or condition and which did not require any further act or measure for its implementation;

(iii) That its function was to impose a limitation on the power of member states to implement a provision which went contrary to one of the fundamental principles of the Treaty in favour of individuals, i.e. the freedom of movement for workers.

However, the Court of Justice decided that the Home Secretary had power to do what he had done because the voluntary act of an individual in associating with a particular organisation, which involved participation in its activities and identification with its aims, could properly be regarded as a matter of 'personal conduct' within Art. 3(1) of Directive 64/221. A member state was therefore permitted under Art. 48 of the Treaty and Art. 3(1) of the Directive to prohibit, on the grounds of public policy, an individual from entering its territory where the individual was associated with an organisation which the member state considered to be socially harmful and the individual was proposing to enter the territory of the member state in order to take up employment with that organisation. It was immaterial that the organisation was not subject to any restrictions under the law of the member state and that nationals of that state were permitted to take up employment with the organisation.

However, apart from cases such as the above, EEC nationals are admitted freely in order to work and can obviously move freely within the EEC. They can take UK jobs without a permit but must report to the police. They may be deported subject to EEC directives on this matter.

(f) **Non-patrial Commonwealth citizens (without a UK grandparent).** These are citizens of Commonwealth countries who are not UK-descended and include East African asians who hold UK passports and Gibraltarians. They have no right to enter and stay in the UK, nor can they move freely within the EEC except for UK citizens from Gibraltar. They must have a work permit before they can take work here and they can be deported.

(g) **Others.** These are citizens of independent non-Commonwealth and non-EEC countries. They have no right to enter and stay in the UK nor can they move freely within the EEC. They cannot take UK jobs without a permit and must report regularly to the police. They can be deported.

Disabled persons

There is legislation governing the employment of disabled persons. It is contained in the Disabled Persons (Employment) Acts of 1944 and 1958, and s 1 of the 1944 Act defines a disabled person as a person who on account of injury, disease, or congenital deformity, is substantially handicapped in obtaining or keeping employment, or in undertaking work on his own account, of a kind which apart from that injury, disease or deformity would be suited to his age, experience and qualifications. Disabled persons may register as such on a register maintained by the Secretary of State for Employment.

In general terms employers of 20 or more persons are required to maintain a quota of employees who are registered as disabled (1944 Act, s 9). The quota is dealt with by s 10 of the 1944 Act and is usually 3 per cent of the workforce, but this may be varied up or down by Ministerial Orders according to whether an industry is particularly suitable for disabled persons or would be particularly difficult for them to work in.

The law does not actually force an employer to employ disabled persons. The penalties involved for an employer who does not meet his quota are that it is an offence for him to employ additional labour if that would mean that he had less than his quota of disabled persons, or to dismiss a disabled employee without reasonable cause so that after doing so the employer is below his quota. (1944 Act, s 9(2) (5) and (6).)

Employees of the Crown

Reference will be made in dealing with specific aspects of employment law to the position of employees of the Crown. However, certain basic principles of employment law as they relate to Crown employees are considered now.

Contracts of employment

Here the position is as follows:

(i) **Military personnel.** Military personnel cannot successfully claim against the Crown for breach of contract (*Dickson* v. *Combermere*, (1863), 3 F. and F. 527) nor can they claim arrears of pay (*Leaman* v. *R.*, [1920] 3 K.B. 663).

(ii) **Civil servants.** At common law civil servants are dismissable at pleasure (*Shenton* v. *Smith*, [1895] A.C. 229) but can claim arrears of pay (*Kodeeswaran* v. *A.G. of Ceylon*, [1970] 2 WLR 456). Furthermore, *dicta* in *Reilly* v. *R.*, [1934] A.C. 176 suggest that even at common law an express promise to employ for a definite period, the contract to be determinable only 'for cause', e.g. misconduct, overrides the implied term relating to dismissal of civil servants at pleasure. However, the provisions of the Employment Protection (Consolidation) Act, 1978, which protect employees against unfair dismissal, apply to civil servants but not to military personnel.

Actions in tort

Actions in tort will lie against the Crown for the torts of its employees or agents committed in the course of their employment; for breach of duty owed at common law by an employer to his employees and for breaches of statutory duties, e.g. breaches of the duty to fence dangerous machines under safety legislation.

Indemnity, contribution and contributory negligence

The law as to indemnity and contribution under the Law Reform (Married Women and Tortfeasors) Act, 1935 applies to Crown cases so that if the Crown is a joint tortfeasor it can claim a contribution or indemnity as the case may be from fellow wrongdoers. In addition the Law Reform (Contributory Negligence) Act, 1945 also applies to Crown cases.

Immunities

No action lies in tort against the Crown or the individual Crown employee for anything done or omitted to be done in relation to any postal packet, telephone communication or telegram, though an action will lie for damages for loss of a registered inland postal packet.

It should be noted that the Post Office Act, 1969 established the Post Office as a public authority which is not an agent of the Crown and does not enjoy the immunities and privileges of the Crown. Nevertheless, the immunities outlined above still apply being contained in ss 29 and 30 of the Act of 1969. These sections were raised in *Harold Stephen & Co. Ltd* v. *Post Office*, [1977] 1 WLR 1172, where the Court of Appeal refused to grant an injunction against the Post Office to companies in the Cricklewood area of London whose business was in jeopardy because they were receiving no mail through the Post Office's action in closing the local sorting office and suspending Post Office workers refusing to handle mail in support of workers employed in the private sector as part of the Grunwick dispute. The Court said that the Act of 1969 put the Post Office in a privileged position by making it immune against actions in contract and tort except for registered letters.

Both the Crown and any member of the armed forces are immune from liability in tort in respect of the death of, or personal injury to another member of the armed forces on duty, provided that the death or injury arises out of military service which ranks for the purpose of pension.

FORMATION — WRITTEN PARTICULARS

The common law does not require any written formalities for a contract of employment. Legislation does sometimes impose a requirement of writing. Reference has already been made to the position regarding apprentices (see *Kirkby* v. *Taylor*, p. 23) and it may be noted here that the Merchant Shipping Act, 1970, s 1 provides that the contract of employment entered into by merchant seamen must be in writing. However, by far the most important requirements in terms of written particulars are contained in the Employment Protection (Consolidation) Act, 1978 (EPCA).

Written Particulars under the EPCA

S 1 of the EPCA requires an employer to give his employee a statement regarding the employment not later than 13 weeks after the employment has commenced.

Contents – generally

The statement must contain the following information:

(i) **The names of the employer and the employee.** A letter of engagement will usually be addressed to the employee and so identify him and the letterheading will identify the employer, though where the employment is with a company which is part of a group care should be taken to state the name of the employing company if the particulars are given by an officer of another company within the group.

(ii) **The date when the employment began.** This is important for the purposes of deciding on the statutory period of notice to be given.

(iii) **Whether the employment counts as a period of continuous employment with previous employment.** This is important because the rights of the employee in terms of unfair dismissal and redundancy depend upon the serving of a period of continuous employment.

As regards previous employments counting as continuous employment, the relevant provisions are contained in Sched. 13 of the EPCA. In general employment will be regarded as continuous if the change of employer was the result of:

(a) a transfer between associated employers. This provision is applicable to transfers of employees from one company in a group to another.

(b) a transfer of the business in which the employee was employed to another person.

(c) a transfer from an employer to his personal representatives because the employer has died.

(d) a change in the partners where the employee is employed by a firm, or a change in personal representatives or trustees where the employee is employed by the estate of a deceased person or by a trust.

A succession of contracts between the same parties are regarded as continuous employment. Thus where a person has been promoted and made a number of new contracts with the same employer, the previous employments are continuous with the present one.

Where previous employments count towards continuous employment the date when the first of those previous employments commenced must be stated.

Contents — terms of the employment

The statement then goes on to set out the terms of employment *as at a specified date* not more than one week before the statement is given. The terms to be set out are:

1. The scale or rate of remuneration or the method of calculating remuneration, as where there are commission or bonus payments.

2. The intervals at which remuneration is paid, i.e. weekly or monthly, and the day or date of payment.

3. Any terms or conditions relating to the hours to be worked, e.g. 'the normal working hours are . . .'

4. Terms relating to holiday entitlement (including accrued holiday pay on termination of service).

5. Terms relating to sickness and injury, including sick pay arrangements.

6. Whether or not there is a pension scheme.

7. Length of notice which the employee must give and the length of notice he is entitled to receive to end the contract. As we shall see later there are *minimum* periods of notice required to terminate contracts of employment and these are set out in s 49 of the EPCA.

8. The title of the job.

If the contract is for a fixed term, e.g. 3 years, the date of termination must be stated.

Contents — disciplinary rules and grievances

Disciplinary procedures deal with, e.g. the number of warnings, oral or written, which will be given before suspension or dismissal. *Grievance procedures* relate to complaints in regard to any aspect of the employment with which the employee is dissatisfied and not merely to disciplinary matters.

The written particulars *may* contain the disciplinary and grievance procedures, though reference may be made in the particulars to a separate document or booklet in which they are contained. However, the particulars *must* state the person to whom the employee may apply if he is not satisfied with a disciplinary decision or has a grievance.

Disciplinary rules relating to health and safety at work must under s 2(3) of the Health and Safety at Work Act, 1974 be given in a separate document which sets out the employer's health and safety policy. This document is often given with the particulars of employment.

Before leaving the matter of written particulars mention should be made of s 1(4) (d) of the EPCA under which the particulars must state whether the employer has contracted out of the Social Security Pensions Act, 1975.

Changes in the terms of the contract

Under s 4, EPCA if the terms of the contract are changed the employee must be notified in writing within one month of the change either by a statement which is left with the employee or a reasonably accessible notice.

If in the original particulars reference is made to a document in which future changes in terms are to be recorded, then an employer who includes changes in that document within one month of their being made need not give written notice to each employee.

In an organisation which does not have collective agreements negotiated with trade unions a variation of the contract may not be accepted by the employee and, unless he accepts, the employer is in breach of contract by introducing the variation. In such a situation it is a matter of good practice that the employee should be required to sign a copy of the document recording the change so that he cannot afterwards say that he did not receive notification of the change or agree to the change. Where terms of employment are regulated by collective agreements the original particulars given to the employee should refer to this. If this is done the effect will normally be that any new terms negotiated under a collective agreement will be deemed to be incorporated into the contract without the consent of the employee (and see p. 118).

Failure to comply with the written particulars obligations

Under s 11 EPCA, if an employer fails to give written particulars, or adequate written particulars at the start of the employment, or fails to notify changes in the terms of the contract, the employee may refer the matter to an industrial tribunal. In addition, if a statement is given but its adequacy is disputed by the employee, then the employer or employee may refer the matter to an industrial tribunal. The tribunal may then, as appropriate, make a declaration that the employee has a right to a statement and what particulars should be included in it or amended within it. The statement approved by the tribunal in its decision is then deemed to have been given by the employer to the employee and will form the basis of his rights.

Although the matter has not been fully worked out by the courts, failure to give written particulars would not seem to render the contract unenforceable by the parties nor would the fact that a change in terms is not notified necessarily mean that the new term was not enforceable if there was other evidence of the change of a term and its acceptance by the employee (*Parkes Classic Confectionery* v. *Ashcroft*, [1973] I.T.R. 43).

Exemptions from written particulars requirements

The EPCA provides that in some situations the employer is not required to comply with the written particulars requirements. In broad terms these are as follows:

(a) An employee who leaves his job but comes back within six months on the same terms and conditions need not be given a statement on his return provided he had one on the occasion of his first employment. (S 2(4), ECPA.)

(b) Employees whose hours of employment are usually less than 16 hours, (s 3, EPCA) — but eight hours in some situations (see s 146, EPCA).

(c) The particulars provisions do not apply if an employee is given a copy of a written contract of employment, the terms of which give all the necessary particulars (s 5, EPCA).

(d) Crown employees, such as civil servants, are excluded (s 138, EPCA).

(e) The rules do not apply to a person whose work is wholly or mainly outside Great Britain (s 141, EPCA).

(f) Mariners on certain ships and fishing boats are excluded (s 144, EPCA), as are registered dock workers (s 145, EPCA).

(g) There is no need for written particulars where the employee is the husband or wife of the employer (s 146, EPCA).

Finally, it is, of course, not necessary to give an employee written particulars where he leaves the employment within 13 weeks of its commencement.

FORMATION – RECRUITMENT AND SELECTION

A number of statutory restrictions on the recruitment and selection of employees and the terms offered to them apply and are considered below.

Discrimination on Grounds of Sex, Marital Status or Race

The relevant provisions of the Sex Discrimination Act, 1975 and the Race Relations Act, 1976 are set out below.

Offers of employment

It is unlawful for a person in relation to an employment by him at a place in England, Wales, or Scotland to discriminate against men or women on grounds of sex marital status, colour, race, nationality or ethnic or national origins:

(i) in the arrangements he makes for the purpose of deciding who should be offered the job; or
(ii) in the terms on which the job is offered; or
(iii) by refusing or deliberately omitting to offer the job.

'Arrangements' is a wide expression covering a range of recruitment techniques, e.g. asking an employment agency to send only white applicants or male applicants. Discrimination by employment agencies is also covered.

As regards the terms of the contract of employment, it is unlawful to discriminate against an employee on the grounds listed above in terms of the employment which is given to him or the terms of access to opportunities for promotion, transfer or training, or to any other benefit, facilities or services, or subjecting him to any other detriment. Thus it is unlawful to discriminate in regard to matters such as privileged loans and mortgages by banks and building societies and discounts on holidays given to employees of travel firms.

A person who takes on workers supplied by a third party rather than employing them himself is obliged by the Acts not to discriminate in the treatment of them or in the work they are allowed to do. Thus temporary staff supplied by an agency are covered by the anti-discrimination provisions.

The anti-discrimination provisions are also extended to partnerships as regards failure to offer a partnership or the terms on which it is offered, including benefits, facilities and services. The provision applies only to firms of six or more partners although there is a power in the legislation to reduce this number. The provision as it stands will allow discrimination in the majority of medical practices but not in major accounting firms. The provisions also cover discrimination in cases where persons are preparing to form themselves into a partnership.

Exceptions

There are some circumstances in which it is lawful to discriminate, and these will now be considered.

POEL—4 **

(a) **Genuine occupational qualifications**. So far as sex discrimination is concerned an employer may confine a job to a man where male sex is a 'genuine occupational qualification' (GOQ) for a particular job. This could arise, for example, for reasons of physiology, as in modelling male clothes, or authenticity in entertainment, as where a part calls for an actor and not an actress. Sometimes a man will be required for reasons of decency or privacy, such as an attendant in a men's lavatory. Sometimes statutory regulations will require the employment of a man, as in the case of night work in a factory where women may not lawfully do such work. Sometimes, too, where the job involves work outside the United Kingdom in a country whose laws and customs would make it difficult for a woman to carry out the job being a male may be a GOQ. As regards marital status, it may be reasonable to discriminate in favour of a man or woman where the job is one of two held by a married couple, as where a woman is a housekeeper living in with her husband who is employed as a gardener.

As regards race, it is lawful to discriminate where there is a GOQ for the job, as, for example, in the employment of a West Indian social worker or probation officer to deal with problems relating to young West Indians. Other instances are dramatic performances or other entertainment, artists or photographic models and employment in places serving food or drink to be purchased *and consumed* on the premises by the public. Thus being Chinese is a GOQ for employment in a Chinese restaurant, but not necessarily in a 'takeaway'.

(b) **Other major exceptions**. These are as follows:
(i) *Private households and small firms*. Sex and marital discrimination is not unlawful where the employment is in a private household or where the employer has not more than five employees. Part-timers count as full employees and all the employer's establishments, if more than one, must be counted, so if he has, say, three establishments, each employing three workers, he is not within the exception and must not discriminate. Race discrimination is only lawful in respect of employment in private households.
(ii) *Work outside Great Britain*. The Sex Discrimination Act does not apply to work which is done wholly or mainly outside Great Britain. However, it does apply to work on a British ship, aircraft or hovercraft unless the work is wholly outside Great Britain.
(iii) *Special cases*. The anti-discriminatory rules apply to Crown appointments but the provisions regarding sex discrimination do not apply to the armed forces and women are still prevented by the Mines and Quarries Act, 1954 from being employed in a job where the duties ordinarily require the employee to spend a significant of time below ground in an active mine. In general terms service with the police is covered by anti-discrimination provi-

sions, as is service in H.M. prisons. In addition, the legal barriers to men becoming midwives have been removed.

Types of Discrimination

There are two forms of discrimination as follows:

(a) **Direct discrimination**, as where, for example, an employer refuses on grounds of sex or race to grant a suitably qualified person an interview for a job. In addition segregation of workers once in employment on the grounds of sex or race is also unlawful direct discrimination.

(b) **Indirect discrimination**, as where an employer has applied requirements or conditions to a job with which only a considerably smaller number of women than of men can comply.

An example is provided by *Price* v. *The Civil Service Commission*, [1977] I.R.L.R. 291: Employment Appeal Tribunal. The Civil Service required candidates for the position of executive officer to be aged between 17½ and 28 years. Belinda Price complained that this age bar constituted indirect sex discrimination against women because women between those ages were more likely than men to be temporarily out of the labour market having children or caring for children at home. It was held by the Employment Appeal Tribunal that the age bar was indirect discrimination against women. The Court held that the words 'can comply' must not be construed narrowly. It could be said that any female applicant could comply with the condition in the sense that she was not obliged to marry or to have children or to look after them — indeed she may find someone else to look after them or, as a last resort, put them into care. If the legislation was construed in that way it was no doubt right to say that any female applicant could comply with the condition. However, in the view of the Court to construe the legislation in that way appeared to be wholly out of sympathy with the spirit and intention of the Act. A person should not be deemed to be able to do something merely because it was theoretically possible; it was necessary to decide whether it was possible for the person to do so in practice as distinct from theory.

Remedies

The remedies or sanctions available against an employer who has contravened the anti-discrimination requirements will be considered in more detail when we come to look at conciliation and industrial tribunals. However, it will perhaps suffice to say for the moment that allegations of discrimination may be the subject of a complaint to an industrial tribunal which may, among other things, award monetary compensation.

In addition the Equal Opportunities Commission which is responsible for keeping under review the working of sex discrimination legislation, including equal pay, and the Commission for Racial Equality, which has a similar function in terms of racial discrimination, may carry out formal investigations into firms where discrimination is alleged and may issue non-discrimination notices requiring the employer to comply with the relevant legislation.

The employer may appeal to an industrial tribunal within six weeks of service of the notice. If there is no appeal, or the industrial tribunal confirms the notice, then the employer must comply with it and if he does not the relevant commission may ask the county court for an injunction which, if granted, will render an employer who ignores it in contempt of court and he may be fined and/or imprisoned for that offence.

The commissions are also required to enter non-discrimination notices which have become final in a register. Copies of the register are kept in Manchester (Equal Opportunities Commission) and in London (Commission for Racial Equality) and are available for inspection to any person on payment of a fee and copies may also be obtained.

Relationship between the Sex Discrimination Act and Equal Pay Act

The Equal Pay Act, 1970 will be considered later when the duties of an employer with regard to remuneration are dealt with. However, it should be noted that the Act of 1970 provides for an individual woman or man to be treated not less favourably than another man or woman in the same employment in respect of pay and other terms of the contract of employment where those involved are employed on the same work, or on work which is broadly similar, or on work which has been given an equal value under a job evaluation exercise. The EPA and the SDA do not overlap. Complaints of discrimination in regard to pay and other non-monetary matters governed by the contract of employment such as hours of work are dealt with under the EPA and complaints of discrimination in regard, e.g. to access to jobs, are dealt with under the SDA. A complaint to an industrial tribunal need not be based from the beginning on one Act or the other. An industrial tribunal is empowered to make a decision under whichever Act turns out to be relevant when all the facts are before it. Nevertheless, there are cases in which the existence of two Acts, as distinct from a single all-embracing statute such as the Race Relations Act, 1976, can give rise to difficulties (see p. 56).

Rehabilitation of Offenders

The provisions of the Rehabilitation of Offenders Act, 1974 are an attempt to give effect to the principle that when a person convicted of crime has been successful in living down that conviction and has avoided further criminal activities, common justice demands that his efforts should not be prejudiced by the unwarranted disclosure of that earlier conviction.

All sentences are subject to rehabilitation except:

(a) Imprisonment for life;

(b) Imprisonment or corrective training for a term exceeding 30 months;

(c) Preventive detention and sentences of detention passed under s 53 of the Children and Young Persons Act, 1933 if the detention was to be during Her Majesty's pleasure or for a term exceeding 30 months.

Corrective training and preventive training were abolished in England and Wales by s 27(1) of the Criminal Justice Act, 1967 but it is necessary to provide for them in relation to living persons who have served such sentences. Furthermore, the Children and Young Persons Act, 1933 s 53 (as amended by the Criminal Justice Act, 1961) provides for the detention during Her Majesty's pleasure of persons convicted of murder who appear to have been under 18 at the time of commission of the offence and for the detention at the discretion of the Secretary of State of children and young persons convicted of offences carrying more than four years' imprisonment.

Subject to what is said above, the rehabilitation period for other sentences depends upon the particular sentence imposed. Thus by Table A, which appears in s 5 of the Act, the rehabilitation period, if it was a sentence of imprisonment or corrective training for a term exceeding six months but not exceeding 30 months, is ten years; if it was for a period not exceeding six months, it is seven years; or, if the sentence was a fine it is five years. Moreover, in these cases if the person convicted was at the date of the conviction under 17 the rehabilitation periods are half of those stated.

Table B, which is also in s 5 of the Act, covers the rehabilitation periods for certain sentences on younger offenders. For example, for Borstal training it is seven years, for detention at a detention centre it is three years. In addition to Tables A and B various other rehabilitation periods are also covered by s 5. For example, the rehabilitation period for an absolute discharge is six months and for a conditional discharge or probation it is one year, or the end of the period when the order ceases to have effect, whichever is the longer. If more than one sentence is imposed in respect of a person, the rehabilitation period applicable is the longest for any of the sentences imposed.

So far as the employment of persons with previous convictions is concerned, it should be noted that any questions seeking information as to a person's previous convictions shall be treated as not relating to spent convictions and a person seeking employment is not required to disclose a spent conviction, and a spent conviction or failure to disclose a spent conviction is not a proper ground for dismissal or excluding a person from, or prejudicing him in, any occupation, office, profession, or employment.

The provisions of the Act apply to convictions, whether by courts in Great Britain or outside, and they also apply to persons dealt with in service disciplinary proceedings.

Trade Union Membership

It is lawful for an employer to make it a condition of employment that the employee shall be a member of a trade union or staff association. Furthermore, there seems to be no legal reason why an employer should not make non-membership of a trade union a condition of employment.

However, once the employment has commenced the EPCA gives certain statutory rights in regard to trade union membership and activities. These are dealt with later when considering rights and duties under the contract of employment (see p. 63).

Discriminatory Advertisements for Employees

The SDA and the RRA make it unlawful to place advertisements for employees which are discriminatory unless they relate to a recognised exceptional case, as where, for example, there is a GOQ. Thus job descriptions such as waiter, salesgirl, stewardess, or 'girl Friday' have largely disappeared from our newspapers and one now finds the descriptions waiter/waitress, or the inclusion 'male/female' as indicating that both sexes are eligible for employment. However, one still sees advertisements which are clearly intended to attract female applicants which nevertheless remain within the law, e.g. 'Publishing Director requires a sophisticated PA/secretary with style and charm who can remain cool under pressure'.

Before legislation relating to discrimination came into force advertisements in the UK were discriminatory mainly as regards sex but obviously an advertisement which said 'Chinese only' would be unlawful unless there was a GOQ as, for example, there would be where the advertisement was for a waiter in a Chinese restaurant.

As regards sanctions, the placing of discriminatory advertisements may lead to the issue of a non-discriminatory notice by the appropriate Commission which, if not complied with, may lead to proceedings being taken by the Commission in an industrial tribunal. If the industrial tribunal accepts the contention of discrimination and yet the advertiser does not comply but continues to advertise in a discriminatory way, the Commission may take proceedings in the county court for, amongst other things, an injunction, and if this is not complied with the advertiser is in contempt of court and may be punished by fine or imprisonment until he complies.

In addition, it is a criminal offence to place a discriminatory advertisement and those who do may be tried by magistrates and are subject to a fine. The person who publishes the advertisement, e.g. a newspaper proprietor, also commits a criminal offence. However, he may not know precisely that the advertisement is discriminatory. For example, without a knowledge of the advertiser's business he cannot really know whether there is a GOQ or not. Accordingly, he is given a defence to any criminal charge if he can show that in publishing the advertisement:

(a) he relied on a statement by the person placing it to the effect that it was not unlawful and on the face of it it might come within one of the exceptional cases, and

(b) it was reasonable for him to rely on that statement.

RIGHTS AND DUTIES OF THE PARTIES TO THE CONTRACT

Duties of Employer

The duties of an employer are an amalgam of common law principles and statutory provisions and may be considered under the headings which follow.

Remuneration

Generally. The rate or amount of pay is decided as follows:

(a) by the contract of employment;

(b) by the terms of a collective agreement made between one or more trade unions and one or more employers' associations, whose terms are incorporated into individual contracts of employment;

(c) by some special machinery for negotiation or statutory authority, e.g. wages councils and teachers' pay.

The pay which is to be received is in nearly all cases definite because it is stated in the written particulars which the EPCA requires the employer to give to the employee (see p. 37) and also because of the provisions of the same Act in relation to itemised pay statements (see p. 53).

However, in the unlikely event of there being no express provision for remuneration, the court will normally imply a term into the contract of employment to pay a reasonable remuneration called a *quantum meruit* (how much he has deserved).

The principles of *quantum meruit* are applied also:

(i) where the contract of employment is void. Thus in *Craven-Ellis* v. *Canons Ltd*, [1936] 2 KB 403 the plaintiff was employed as managing director by the company under a contract of employment under seal which provided for remuneration. The articles of the company provided that directors must have qualification shares, and must obtain these within two months of appointment. The plaintiff and other directors did not obtain the required number of shares so that the contract of employment was invalid. However, the plaintiff did give his services to the company for a period of time and he now sued on a *quantum meruit* for a reasonable sum by way of remuneration. It was held that his claim succeeded, there being no valid contract which could provide for remuneration.

(ii) To additional remuneration over and above the basic pay fixed by the contract. Thus in *Powell* v. *Braun*, [1954] 1 WLR 401 an employer wrote to his secretary saying that instead of giving her a rise in salary he would pay her an unspecified bonus on the net trading profits of the previous year. It was held by the Court of Appeal that this amounted to an undertaking to pay the secretary a reasonable sum as a bonus.

However, the concept of *quantum meruit* will not be used to overcome the express terms of a contract. Thus in *Re Richmond Gate Property Co. Ltd*, [1964] 3 All E.R. 936 the company was incorporated on 19 January 1962 and a resolution for a voluntary winding up was passed on 20 September 1962. Walker, one of the two joint managing directors, lodged proof of a salary claim which the liquidator rejected. Walker was appointed on terms that he should receive 'such remuneration as the directors may determine' and in fact the directors had not fixed any remuneration. Nevertheless, Walker claimed £400 either in contract or on a *quantum meruit*. It was held by Mr Justice Plowman in the High Court that the liquidator was right to reject the proof. There could be no claim under the contract because that was only for 'such remuneration as the directors may determine' and none had been determined in this way. Moreover the existence of an express contract in regard to remuneration automatically excluded a claim on a *quantum meruit*.

Holidays and holiday pay. Again, entitlement depends upon the express terms of the contract of service, or the terms of a collective agreement, or a statutory provision such as s 94 of the Factories Act, 1961 which requires those who employ women and young persons in factories to give them Bank Holidays.

There should be no doubt about the entitlement to holidays and holiday pay since the EPCA requires particulars to be given to employees sufficient to enable the precise calculation of entitlement and this includes the amount of accrued holiday pay which will be paid when the employment ends.

Sick pay. The entitlement to sick pay is again a matter which must be dealt with by the employment particulars under the EPCA. However, there is no obligation to provide sick pay except during a statutory period of notice when the employer must pay an employee who is sick and unable to work out all or part of the notice. (S 50 and Sched. 3, EPCA.) (See further p. 104.)

The court may imply a term relating to sick pay and, indeed, in modern law there seems to be a presumption in favour of the employee being entitled to sick pay so that an employer must bring evidence to show that this is not the case.

ORMAN v. SAVILLE SPORTSWEAR LTD, [1960] 3 All E.R. 105: High Court

Facts

The plaintiff was employed at a skirt factory as a production manager. His pay was £30 a week and he took a bonus of 2d for each skirt that was made and this bonus produced a further £20 per week. He had a written contract which did not deal with the matter of wages during sickness. However, the plaintiff was absent through sickness for a number of weeks and when he came back to work he claimed a payment for the period during which he was absent.

Judgment

Mr Justice Pilcher held that since the contract did not deal with the matter, wages were payable during sickness unless the employer could show a contrary intention, which the defendants had not been able to do in this case. Therefore the plaintiff was entitled to pay for his absence during sickness which was assessed at £50 per week.

Comment

The employer may, of course, be able to show that he does not pay wages during sickness to those employed in a capacity similar to that of the plaintiff. Thus in *Petrie* v. *MacFisheries Ltd*, [1940] 1 KB 258, it was held that an employee was only entitled to half pay during a period of sickness where there was a notice at the place of employment that half pay up to a total of 21 days a year would be paid as a matter of grace during illness. Again, in *O'Grady* v. *Saper Ltd*, [1942] KB 469 an employee was held not to be entitled to sick pay where he had been ill on several previous occasions and had not asked for nor been paid any wages. MacKinnon, L.J. said that there was abundant evidence that the employers did not make payments during sickness. He said: 'Conclusive evidence of that is furnished by the fact that on at least three occasions during the time he had been employed he was not paid wages when he was away sick, and he acquiesced in that position.'

Finally, it should be noted that receipt of Social Security sickness benefit does not, as such, prevent a claim for sick pay unless the contract expressly so provides. (*Marrison v. Bell*, [1939] 2 KB 187.)

Pay during suspension

(a) *On medical grounds.* Under s 19, EPCA an employee of not less than four weeks' continuous service who is suspended from work under the provisions of an Act of Parliament such as the Health and Safety at Work Act, 1974 or a code of practice, normally on the advice of a Employment Medical Adviser, not because he is ill but because he may become ill if he continues at work since he is engaged in an industrial process involving a potential health hazard to him, is entitled to be paid normal wages while suspended for up to 26 weeks. Under s 20, EPCA an employee cannot claim suspension payments in respect of periods during which he cannot work by reason of disease or bodily or mental disablement. Where this is so he must fall back on any entitlement to sick pay or sickness or industrial injuries benefits as he may have. In addition, under s 19, there can be no claim to payment on suspension in respect of any period during which the employer has offered to provide suitable alternative work and the employee has unreasonably refused to perform it.

As regards the amount of pay, this is determined under Sched. 14, Part II of the EPCA and will be dealt with later when we come to consider the matter of remuneration during statutory time off (see p. 52). Of course, if the employer continues to pay wages under the contract of employment, these are set off against the employee's statutory entitlement.

As regards sanctions, an employee may present a complaint to an industrial tribunal under s 22 of the EPCA that his employer has failed to pay the whole or any part of remuneration to which he is entitled on suspension, and the tribunal may order the employer to pay the employee the remuneration due to him.

(b) *On disciplinary grounds.* Suspension from work may form part of the disciplinary procedures in a particular employment. There is in general no implied right to suspend an employee for disciplinary purposes without pay. Thus in *Hanley v. Pease & Partners Ltd*, [1915] 1 KB 698 an employee took a day off without permission and his employers suspended him for a further day. It was held that the employee could recover damages from his employers because they had stopped him from earning a day's pay. The employee was, of course, in breach of contract and his employers could have sued him for damages but they were not entitled to quantify those damages through suspension.

In practice, if an employer wishes to suspend without pay, there should be an express term in the contract of employment and this must appear in the EPCA statement giving particulars of the employment or in a fully written contract of employment where such exists.

Suspension for a period which is longer than the notice to which the employee is entitled may operate as a dismissal with an option to return to work, though in such a case the employee is not obliged to return. (*Marshall* v. *English Electric Ltd*, [1945] 1 All E.R. 653.)

Maternity pay. The relevant provisions are contained in ss 33 — 48 of the EPCA and are broadly as follows:

(a) *Maternity pay.* Women who are absent because of pregnancy are, if they have completed two years' service and been at work up to the eleventh week before the expected week of confinement, entitled to maternity pay from their employers. The maternity pay is paid for the first six weeks of absence and is in each week nine-tenths of a week's pay, less the amount of the standard rate of maternity allowance even if the particular employee is not in receipt of this.

The employee must, at least three weeks beforehand or as soon as possible thereafter, tell her employer that she will be absent, and he may require her to produce a medical certificate showing the expected week of confinement.

Employers may claim a rebate for the full amount of maternity pay from a maternity pay fund set up by the Act and financed by an addition of 0.05 per cent to the employer's Social Security contributions and employers may complain to an industrial tribunal if the rebate is not paid.

(b) *Return to work.* If a woman returns to her job within 29 weeks after her baby is born, she must be given back her old job or a suitable alternative. However, she must have informed her employer (in writing, if he requires) of her intention to return at the time she notified him that she was going to be absent to have a baby. She must notify her employer at least one week before she intends to return, and the employer may postpone her return by up to four weeks, as may the employee if she provides a medical certificate giving reasons.

Temporary replacements must be told at the start that the job is temporary, and there is no unfair dismissal of the temporary on the return of the original employee if the method of dismissal is reasonable.

(c) *Failure to make a payment.* An employee may present a complaint to an industrial tribunal that her employer has failed to pay the whole or any part of maternity pay due, and may question its amount. The tribunal may order the employer to pay the employee the amount of maternity pay which the tribunal finds is due to her. If she cannot recover payment, as where the employer will not pay or is insolvent, the employee may apply to the Secretary of State who will pay her what is due out of the Maternity Pay Fund. The Secretary of State may then recover such an amount from the employer as the Secretary of State thinks reasonable, not exceeding the amount the employer has failed to pay.

Where an employer will not take back a woman after absence for maternity leave she will be treated as dismissed from the notified date of return. Then she may be treated as redundant or unfairly dismissed, and may pursue remedies on that basis (see p. 92).

Pay during lay-off — guarantee payments
(a) *Lay-off.* To avoid difficulties the right to lay-off employees without pay because of lack of work should be made an express term of the contract. However, even where this has been done the employer's rights are restricted by statutory provisions which provide for guarantee payments.
(b) *Guarantee payments.* Under the provisions of ss 12-18 of the EPCA employees with not less than four weeks' continuous service are entitled to a guarantee payment up to a maximum of £7.25 per day if they are not provided with work on a normal working day. This guarantee is limited to five days in any calendar quarter, starting on the first days of February, May, August, and November, i.e. an absolute maximum of 20 days per year.

The provisions do not apply if the failure to provide work is due to a trade dispute, or if the employee has been offered suitable alternative work but has refused it.

The Secretary of State for Employment is given power in the EPCA to give exemption by statutory instrument from the guarantee payments provisions where there is a collective agreement or an order of a wages council which provides for guarantee payments which are satisfactory to the Secretary of State. Application for exemption may be made by the trade unions and employers who are parties to the collective agreement or by the particular wages council involved.

An employee may present a complaint to an industrial tribunal that his employer has failed to pay the whole or any part of a guarantee payment to which the employee is entitled. This industrial tribunal may make an order to pay the employee the amount of guarantee payment which it finds is due to him.

Pay during statutory time off. The EPCA, ss 27-32 give employees certain rights to time off work. These will be more fully considered later (see p. 64). However, in two cases the employee is, in addition, entitled to pay during the time off and these situations are dealt with here as part of the law relating to remuneration. The two cases are:

(a) *Time off for carrying out trade union duties.* An employer must allow an employee who is an official of an independent trade union recognised by the employer to take time off during working hours for the purpose of carrying out his duties as a trade union official where those duties are concerned with industrial relations between his employer and any associated employer and their employees, or to take training in aspects of industrial relations which are relevant to the carrying out of his duties and in addition are approved by the Trades Union Congress or by the independent trade union of which the employee is an official.

Obviously, these provisions will require some interpretation in the practical situation and the Advisory, Conciliation and Arbitration Service has published a code of practice entitled 'Time off for Trade Union Duties and Activities' which gives guidance on the matter. The code is available from Government bookshops and other booksellers.

(b) *Redundant employees.* An employee who has been continuously employed by his employer for at least two years and who is given notice of dismissal because of redundancy is entitled before the period of his notice expires to reasonable time off during working hours so that he may look for new employment or make arrangements for training for future employment.

As regards the amount of money which is payable, there are statutory formulae. For trade union duties, the pay is calculated as the amount the employee would have received if he had spent the time off at work where he is paid solely with reference to time. Where the employee is paid partly by reference to the amount of work done, payment is arrived at by applying the employee's average hourly earnings rate to the time spent off work.

In the case of time off to look for work or to make arrangements for training on redundancy, the remuneration is calculated by dividing the amount of a week's pay (as defined by Sched. 14, Part II of the EPCA) by the number of normal working hours in the week (as defined by Sched. 14, Part I of the EPCA).

As regards sanctions, the employee may complain to an industrial tribunal if the employer fails to make a payment as required and an industrial tribunal may, if the complaint is substantiated, order the payment to be made.

Itemised pay statements. Under ss 8-10 of the EPCA an employer must give his employees an itemised pay statement. Before the enactment of these provisions an employer could simply state the amount of take-home pay without more. Now there must be a statement showing gross pay and take-home pay and the variable deductions, e.g. income tax, which make up the difference between the two figures. As regards fixed deductions, e.g. savings, these need not be itemised every pay day. If the employer gives the employee a statement setting out the fixed deductions he may simply show a lump sum representing these in the weekly/monthly pay statement. This fixed deduction statement must be updated in writing if it is changed and in any case it must be reissued every 12 months.

There are some exceptions where an itemised pay statement need not be given. These are (a) where the employee is the spouse of the employer; (b) where the work is outside Great Britain; (c) where the employment is for less than 16 hours per week; and (d) in the case of merchant seamen and share fishermen, i.e. fishermen who are remunerated solely by a share of the profits of the catch.

As regards sanctions, an employee may complain to an industrial tribunal if the employer fails to give him an itemised pay statement and either employer or employee can ask an industrial tribunal to decide what should be included in an itemised pay statement or in the standing statement of fixed deductions. The tribunal will make a declaration that a statement should be given and as to what it should include, and the employer must comply with this declaration. In addition an industrial tribunal may order the employer to give back to the employee any deductions which he made from his pay and which were not notified during the 13 weeks preceeding the date of application to the tribunal.

The method of payment and deductions from pay. This is governed by the Truck Acts, 1831-1940 and the Payment of Wages Act, 1960. The Truck Acts were passed to prevent bad employers:

(a) from paying wages by giving their employees goods or requiring that wages paid be spent at the employer's store; and

(b) from making unreasonable deductions from wages for poor work or for benefits, often of dubious value, which the employer provided.

The need for these rules has, of course, decreased in modern times and they are much less important today. However, the main principles are as follows:

(1) *manual* workers must be paid in cash with no restrictions as to how the wage is to be spent. If goods are supplied in lieu of wages the employee may keep the goods and still make a claim for his wages. However, under the Payment of Wages Act, 1960 the worker may consent in writing to receive payment of wages by cheque or postal order or by payment into a bank.

(2) Deductions from wages for benefits supplied by the employer are

restricted, though deductions may be made for rent of a house supplied by the employer and in regard to food prepared and consumed on the premises by the employee.

(3) Deductions for disciplinary purposes or bad work or damage to material must be fair and reasonable and the employee must consent in writing to the deductions being made or, alternatively, there must be a notice in the workshop explaining the grounds on which and the basis on which deductions are made.

(4) Deductions may be made to pay debts due from the employee to a third party (i.e. not the employer). This covers trade union subscriptions (*Williams* v. *Butlers Ltd*, [1975] 2 All E.R. 889) provided the employee consents to or requests the deduction in writing. Deductions which are requested or consented to in writing are allowed for, e.g. sports clubs, provided, by reason of the Shops Clubs Act, 1902, the club is not controlled by the employer but is, e.g. run by an independent committee.

(5) In some cases an Act of Parliament allows deductions from pay without the consent of the employee. Obvious examples are deductions for income tax under PAYE arrangements and social security contributions. In addition, the Attachment of Earnings Act, 1971 allows the High Court, a County Court, and a Magistrates Court to make an order authorising deductions from pay for a variety of purposes, e.g. non-payment of maintenance to a wife, and ordinary civil debt.

Equal Pay

The Equal Pay Act, 1970 (EPA), as amended by the SDA, 1975, implies a term called an equality clause into contracts of service. This clause requires that a man or woman be given contractual terms not less favourable than those given to an employee of the opposite sex when they are each employed:

(a) *on like work* in the same employment; or

(b) *on work rated as equivalent* in the same employment.

The EPA and the SDA are complementary, the EPA covering not only matters concerning wages and salaries but also other matters governed by the contract of service, including non-monetary terms, e.g. sick pay. Other forms of sex discrimination in employment, e.g. discriminatory advertising and recruitment techniques are covered by the SDA.

However, there are gaps in the legislation which sometimes prevents a remedy being given.

MEEKS v. NATIONAL UNION OF AGRICULTURAL AND ALLIED WORKERS, [1976] I.R.L.R. 198: Industrial Tribunal

Facts

Mrs Meeks was employed by the union as a part-time clerical assistant carrying out secretarial duties. She worked a 23-hour week and was paid 91p per hour. Full-time secretarial workers at the Norwich office where Mrs Meeks worked were all women and received 110p per hour for a 35-hour week. Mrs Meeks claimed that the union's practice contravened the SDA and the EPA.

Judgment

An industrial tribunal found that there was indirect sex discrimination against Mrs Meeks because a part-timer was far more likely to be a woman than a man. However, they were unable to give her a remedy because the complaint was in regard to pay and therefore not within the SDA. In addition, the full-timers on the higher rate of pay were also women and so Mrs Meeks could not claim under the EPA either because a comparison for equal pay must be with a man.

Comment

Problems such as this could be solved by amalgamating the SDA and the EPA into a single Act which included issues relating to pay within its scope. This would remove the present anomaly that the concept of indirect discrimination relates to matters other than pay. The Race Relations Act, 1976 does combine all questions under one piece of legislation.

Application of EPA. The Act applies to all forms of full- and part-time work, whether manual or non-manual. There are no exclusions for small firms or in respect of persons who have only recently taken up the employment. There is no exception in the case of employment on a ship registered in Great Britain, or on an aircraft or hovercraft registered here and operated by a person who has his principal place of business here or is ordinarily resident here, unless the employees do their work *wholly* outside Great Britain.

The armed forces and police are excluded, being subject to separate provisions regarding discriminatory pay which are not considered here.

The Act applies to discrimination against men, though claims are normally made by women, and we shall consider the law on the assumption of a claim by a woman. As we have seen, all alleged unequal contract terms are covered, e.g. sick pay and holiday pay. (And see *NAAFI* v. *Varley*, 1977 p. 58, where the claim related to unequal working hours.)

Main provisions of EPA. These are as follows:

(a) If a woman is engaged in the same or broadly similar work as a man and both are working for the same or an associated employer (see below) the woman is entitled to the same rate of pay and other terms of employment as the man.

It is of interest to note that the comparison may be made with a previous holder of the same job. Thus in *Macarthys* v. *Smith, The Times*, 17 December 1977 the Employment Appeal Tribunal decided that Mrs Smith, a stockroom manageress, was entitled to pay which was equal to that of a previous manager of the stockroom, a Mr McCullough. However, the EAT did say that industrial tribunals must be cautious in making such comparisons unless the interval between the two employments is reasonably short.

(b) If the job which a woman does has been given the same value as a man's job under a job evaluation scheme she is entitled to the same rate of pay and other terms of employment as the man.

Of course, when a job evaluation exercise has been carried out both employees and the employer may challenge it. In this connection it was decided by the EAT in *Green* v. *Broxtowe District Council, The Times* 11 November 1976 that industrial tribunals will, in normal circumstances, be bound by the conclusion of a job evaluation study, if one has been carried out, unless it can be shown that it was based upon a fundamental mistake or error.

Broadly similar work. This expression means that although there may be some differences between the work of the man and of the woman these are not of sufficient practical importance to give rise to a 'material difference' within s 1(3) of the EPA (as amended by the SDA, s 8(1) and Sched. 1, Part 2).

Illustrations of the interpretation of 'material difference' are provided by the following cases:

CAPPER PASS v. LAWTON, [1976] I.R.L.R. 366: Employment Appeal Tribunal

Facts

A female cook who worked a 40-hour week preparing lunches for the directors of Capper was paid a lower rate than two male assistant chefs who worked a 45-hour week preparing some 350 meals a day in Cappers' works canteen. The female cook claimed that by reason of the EPA (as amended) she should be paid at the same rate as the assistant chefs since she was employed on work of a broadly similar nature.

Judgment

It was held by the EAT that if the work done by a female applicant was of a broadly similar nature to that done by a male colleague it should be regarded as being like work for the purposes of the EPA unless there were some practical differences of detail between the two types of job. In this case the EAT decided that the work done by the female cook was broadly similar to the work of the assistant chefs and that the differences of detail were not of practical importance in relation to the terms and conditions of employment. Consequently, the female cook was entitled to be paid at the same rate as her male colleagues.

NAVY, ARMY AND AIR FORCE INSTITUTES v. VARLEY, [1977] 1 All E.R. 840: Employment Appeal Tribunal

Facts

Miss Varley worked as a Grade E clerical worker in the accounts office of NAAFI in Nottingham. NAAFI conceded that her work was like that of Grade E male clerical workers employed in NAAFI's London Office. However, the Grade E workers in Nottingham worked a 37-hour week, while the male Grade E clerical workers in the London office worked a 36½-hour week. Miss Varley applied to an industrial tribunal under the EPA for a declaration that she was less favourably treated as regards hours worked than the male clerical workers in London and that her contract term as to hours be modified so as to reduce it to 36½ hours a week. The industrial tribunal granted that declaration and NAAFI appealed.

Judgment

It was held by the EAT that the variation in hours was genuinely due to a material difference other than the difference of sex. It was due to a real difference in that the male employees worked in London where there was a custom to work shorter hours. Accordingly NAAFI's appeal was allowed and Miss Varley was held not to be entitled to the declaration.

· '. . . There is a geographical distinction between the conditions operated by NAAFI in respect of their employees in London and those outside London. That is by no means a unique situation; it is common to the Civil Service and to all sorts of other employment. . . . In other words, the variation between her contract and a man's contract is due really to the fact that she works in Nottingham and he works in London. It seems to us that it is quite plain that that is the difference between her case and his case, namely that she works in Nottingham where this old custom operates and he works in London where the custom of a shorter working week operates.' (per Phillips, J.)

In some cases different treatment of men and women is allowed on the ground of sensible material differences. Thus, if employee A is a new entrant of 21 and employee B is a long-serving employee of, say, 50, and there is a system of service increments, then it is reasonable to pay B more than A though both are employed on like work.

However, the mere fact that at the present time men are on average paid more than women is not a material difference justifying paying a woman less in a particular job. Thus in *Clay Cross (Quarry Services) Ltd* v. *Fletcher*, [1978] 1 WRL 1429 the company had managed to satisfy the EAT that a male employee was being justifiably paid some £8 a week more than Mrs Fletcher, though both did the same work, on the grounds that he had been earning this larger sum in his previous employment and would not have joined the company for less. The Court of Appeal overruled the decision of the EAT and said that Mrs Fletcher was entitled to the same pay as the man if, as here, she was doing the same job, i.e. sales clerk. The Court said that the employer could not justify on the basis of 'material difference' paying her less simply because a subsequent employee was a man and would not take less than the wage he had received in his previous job.

Associated employers. Comparison is normally made with persons working at the same place but persons who work at different places may make comparison provided the employer is the same or is an associated employer, as would be the case with a group of companies, so that for example, workers in subsidiary A might compare themselves with workers in subsidiary B or with workers in the holding company, provided that there are common terms and conditions of employment across the group.

Central Arbitration Committee. Where pay is based on a collective agreement between unions and employers which specifies different rates for men and women, application may be made to the Central Arbitration Committee (CAC) to amend the agreement to remove discriminatory differences. A Wages Council order, or a particular employer's pay structure fixing common terms for his employees or any class thereof, may be similarly referred.

References to the CAC are made as follows:

(i) collective agreements – by any party to the agreement or by the Secretary of State;

(ii) employers' pay structures — by the employer concerned or by the Secretary of State;

(iii) wages orders — by the Secretary of State.

Individual employees cannot make references to the Committee but they may send details of any agreement or pay structure or order which is potentially discriminatory to the Secretary of State who may consider a possible reference to the CAC.

Reference to industrial tribunal. A complaint of unequal treatment in a job under the EPA may be made to an industrial tribunal at any time while the complainant is still doing the job or within six months after termination of the particular employment. Where there is a disagreement as to equality of treatment between an employer and employee, an employer, instead of merely refusing to consider the matter, may himself apply to an industrial tribunal for an order declaring the rights of the parties. There is a right of appeal from the decision of an industrial tribunal to the Employment Appeal Tribunal by either party on a point of law.

Conciliation. In most cases which come before industrial tribunals (other than redundancy payment cases) provision is made for copies of the relevant documents to be sent to a conciliation officer of the Advisory, Conciliation and Arbitration Service (ACAS), who may try to help the parties to reach a settlement. It should be noted that any information which is given to the conciliation officer for this purpose is not admissible in evidence if there is a subsequent tribunal hearing unless the party who gave the information to the conciliation officer consents.

Restraints on pay. Restraints upon employees' pay have been in operation in one form or another since 1966. It is not proposed to deal with these because they are subject to constant change but obviously they do affect the amount of remuneration payable and the latest provisions, if any, should be ascertained.

Employer's Duty to Provide work

The duty to provide work is more fully considered in the section dealing with the statutory provisions of the EPCA regarding unfair dismissal (see p. 86). However, the position at common law is that there is no duty to provide work so that if an employer continues to pay wages or salary the employee cannot regard the employer as in breach of contract and has no right of action for a lump sum of damages for wrongful dismissal, but must merely accept his pay. The leading case is *Collier* v. *Sunday Referee*, [1940] 2 KB 647, where Asquith, J. said: 'If I pay my cook her wages she cannot complain if I take all my meals out.'

There are exceptions at common law in regard to persons paid by commission or pieceworkers where failure to provide work is regarded as a breach of contract and this is so in the case of actors because they need to keep an image by occasional public performances.

However, as we shall see, in unfair dismissal cases industrial tribunals have been working towards a general right to work and regarding failure to provide work as a dismissal for the purposes of the unfair dismissal provisions of the EPCA.

Employer's Duty in Regard to the Employee's Property

An employer has no duty to protect his employee's property.

DEYONG v. SHENBURN, [1946] 1 All E.R. 226: Court of Appeal

Facts

The plaintiff entered into a contract of employment with the defendant under which the plaintiff was to act the dame in a pantomime for three weeks. Rehearsals took place at a theatre and on the second day the plaintiff had stolen from his dressing room his overcoat as well as two shawls and a pair of shoes forming part of his theatrical equipment. In the county court the judge found that the defendant had been negligent in failing to provide a lock on the dressing room door and in having no-one at the stage door during the morning of the particular rehearsal day to prevent the entry of unauthorised persons. However, the county court judge held that the defendant was under no duty to protect the clothing. The plaintiff appealed to the Court of Appeal where the case proceeded on the ground that a duty was laid on an employer to use care to provide a safe system of working to protect his servant from injury, and that a similar duty applied also in regard to the protection of the employee's property so far as it enabled the employee to do his work and even extended to protection against theft.

Judgment

The plaintiff's contention was rejected by the Court of Appeal which decided that the defendant was not liable. 'I am not deciding that it is so, but it may well be that if, through a breach of the duty to provide a proper system of working, a workman is not only injured in his person but also suffers damage to his clothing, the damage to the clothing can properly be included in the damages. It may be that if, through such a breach, his clothes are torn off his back and he suffers no personal injury he may be entitled to recover damages, but it does not in the least follow from that there is a duty upon the employer, which would be quite a different duty from that which I have mentioned to take steps to safeguard the workman while in his employ against loss through the wrongful act of a third person. That conclusion does not follow as it seems to me, in the least, and cannot be made to follow by any process of reasoning that is not plainly fallacious ...'. (per du Parcq, L.J.)

Comment

This decision was also applied in the later case of *Edwards* v. *West Herts Group Hospital Management Committee*, [1957] 1 All E.R. 541 where the plaintiff, a resident house physician at the defendants' hospital, had had some articles of clothing and personal effects stolen from his bedroom at the hostel where he was required to reside, and brought an action for damages for negligence and breach of an implied duty under his contract of employment. His action was dismissed in the county court and his appeal to the Court of Appeal was also dismissed on the basis that there was no such contractual duty in respect of property.

Employee's Indemnity

The employer is bound to indemnify the employee in regard to expenses, losses and liabilities incurred by the employee during the carrying out of his duties.

RE FAMATINA DEVELOPMENT CORPORATION LTD, [1974] 2 Ch. 271: Court of Appeal

Facts

A company employed a consulting engineer to make a report on its activities. The written report contained matters which the managing director alleged were a libel upon him and he brought an action against the engineer in respect of this on the basis of the publication of the report to the directors of the company, all of whom had received a copy. The managing director's action failed but the engineer incurred costs in defending the claim which he now sought to recover from the company.

Judgment

The Court of Appeal held that the comments made in the report were within the scope of the engineer's employment. His terms of engagement required him to report fully and frankly and in the circumstances he was entitled to the indemnity.

Comment

There is no duty to indemnify an employee against liability for his own negligence. Thus, if by negligence an employee injures a third party in the course of employment and the third party sues the employee, the employer is not required to indemnify the employee and, indeed, if the employer is sued as vicariously liable he has a right to an indemnity against the employee, though the action is unlikely to be brought for reasons already given (see *Lister* v. *Romford Ice & Cold Storage Ltd*, p. 18).

Trade Union Membership and Activities

Under the provisions of the EPCA, ss 23-26, employers may not take action against employees simply because they are members of, or take part, *at an appropriate time* (which extends to activities on the employer's premises *Post Office* v. *Union of Post Office Workers*, *The Times*, 12 December 1973) in the activities of a trade union which is *independent* of the employer.

Nor may action be taken against employees to force them to join a trade union which is not independent or to compel them to join a trade union if they object on religious grounds.

It was held in *Saggers* v. *British Railways Board*, [1977] 1 WLR 1090, Employment Appeal Tribunal, that in considering whether an employee's refusal to join a trade union was because of a genuine objection on the grounds of religious belief, an industrial tribunal should have regard not only to the general creed of the religious sect (in this case Jehovah's Witnesses) to which the employee belongs but also to his own personal beliefs. In this case it appeared that the Jehovah's Witnesses did not object to their members joining trade unions but it was held by the EAT that it was not enough for an industrial tribunal to base its decision on this. They should look at the personal beliefs of the employee concerned and, as he objected on religious grounds, that was enough.

Employees against whom action is taken may complain to an industrial tribunal which in cases not involving dismissal may award compensation or make an order declaring the rights of the employee. Where there is a dismissal the unfair dismissal remedies apply (see p. 90).

Time Off Work

Under the provisions of ss 27-32 of the EPCA employees are entitled to time off work in certain circumstances. Sometimes they are also entitled to pay, as in the case of trade union officials and redundant employees who are looking for work or seeking training for another job. These cases have already been considered as part of the law relating to remuneration (see p. 52).

There are two other cases in which employees are entitled to time off *but the employer is under no obligation to pay them for this*. These are as follows:

(a) **Trade union activities**. An employee who is a member of an independent trade union which the employer recognises is entitled to reasonable time off for trade union activities.

As we have already seen, ACAS has published a code of practice entitled 'Time off for Trade Union Duties and Activities' and this provides guidance on the time off to be permitted by an employer.

(b) **Public duties**. Employers are also required to allow employees who hold certain public positions and offices reasonable time off to carry out the duties which are associated with them.

Details appear in s 29 of the EPCA which covers such offices as Justices of the Peace, members of local authorities, members of any statutory tribunal such as an industrial tribunal, and members of certain health, education, water and river authorities.

Complaints in regard to failure to give time off under (a) and (b) above may be taken to an industrial tribunal. In general, the complaint must be made within three months of the date when the failure to give time off occurred. An industrial tribunal may make an order declaring the rights of the employee to be observed by the employer and may also award monetary compensation to be paid by the employer where there is loss to the employee.

Discrimination once in Employment

We have already considered the law relating to discrimination in formation of the contract of employment (see p. 41) and in terms of remuneration (see p. 55). Discrimination on termination of the contract will be dealt with later when we look at discriminatory dismissals. Here we are concerned with discrimination in the treatment of employees during the course of the contract of employment.

Discrimination on the grounds of sex or race

Under the Sex Discrimination Act, 1975 and the Race Relations Act, 1976 it is unlawful to discriminate against a person on grounds of sex or race as regards opportunities for promotion, training or transfer to other positions, or in the provision of benefits, facilities or services, or by dismissal or any other disadvantages.

However, the EPCA allows women to receive special treatment when they are pregnant, and employers may provide different pension arrangements and retiring ages based on sex. There is no discrimination where the sex or racial status of the employee is a genuine occupational qualification.

There are some exemptions and special cases. Thus the law does not apply to employment for the purposes of a private household or to cases where not more than five persons are employed. In addition, the armed forces are not covered and, as we have seen, the law still prevents women from working as underground miners. These are special provisions relating to midwives and to police and prison officers together with ministers of religion, competitive sports and charities.

There is also an exemption in respect of discriminatory training. An employer or a body responsible for training may provide training exclusively applicable to persons of a particular sex or racial group where the purpose is to enable them to take up work in situations where that sex or racial group is under-represented, but there may not be discrimination in terms of recruitment for such work. Trade unions may also take special action to attract members of particular sexual or racial groups into membership or to office in the union where there is under-representation.

As regards enforcement, if an unlawful act of discrimination is committed by an employee, such as a personnel officer, the employer is held responsible for the act along with the employee unless the employer can show that he took all reasonable steps to prevent the employee from discriminating. If he can do this, only the employee is responsible.

Individual employees who believe they have been discriminated against may make a complaint to an industrial tribunal within three months of the act complained of. It is then the duty of a conciliation officer to see whether the complaint can be settled without going to a tribunal. If, however, a tribunal hears the complaint, it may make an order declaring the rights of the employee and employer in regard to the complaint, the intention being that both parties will abide by the order for the future.

The tribunal may also give the employee monetary compensation, and may additionally recommend that the employer take, within a specified period, action appearing to the tribunal to be practicable for the purpose of obviating or reducing discrimination.

Discrimination against married persons

Under the SDA, 1975 the anti-discriminatory provisions outlined in the previous section are applied also to discrimination against married persons. An employer must not treat a married person of either sex, on the ground of his or her marital status, less favourably than he treats or would treat an unmarried person of the same sex, e.g. there must not be a marriage bar attached to a particular employment.

Victimisation in employment

Under the SDA and the RRA it is unlawful to treat a person less favourably than another because that person has asserted rights under the Equal Pay Act or other anti-discriminatory legislation relating to sex or race, or has helped another person to assert such rights or has given information to the Equal Opportunities Commission or the Commission for Racial Equality or it is thought that he or she *might* do so.

Rehabilitation of offenders

We have already dealt with the provisions of the Rehabilitation of Offenders Act, 1974 (see p. 45) and need only remind ourselves at this point that the fact that a person has a spent conviction is not a ground for prejudicing that person in any occupation or employment.

However, unlike the anti-discriminatory rules relating to sex and race, there are no statutory enforcement proceedings if there is discrimination here. However, a person with a spent conviction who is discriminated against *might* be able to sue for damages in tort on the basis that the employer is in breach of a statutory duty not to prejudice him. As regards actions based on statutory duties, see p. 133.

Testimonials and References

Although as we shall see under s 53, EPCA an employer is now required to give an employee a written statement setting out the reasons for dismissal, there is no legal provision which requires an employer to give a reference or testimonial to an employee or to answer questions or enquiries put to him by a prospective employer. (*Carroll* v. *Bird*, (1800) 3 Esp. 201.) However, if an employer does give a reference or testimonial, either orally or in writing, which is false he commits a criminal offence under the Servants' Characters Act, 1792 and may be liable in damages to certain persons as follows:

(a) **to a subsequent employer** who incurs loss because of a false statement *known* by the former employer to be untrue (*Foster* v. *Charles*, (1830) 7 Bing. 105) or made *negligently* without reasonable grounds for believing the statement to be true, since there is probably a duty of care between the former employer and the subsequent employer. (*Hedley Byrne & Co. Ltd* v. *Heller & Partners Ltd*, [1964] A.C. 465.)

Under the Rehabilitation of Offenders Act there is no liability if an employer fails to disclose a spent conviction to a prospective employer. If an employer does refer to a spent conviction in a testimonial or reference the employee may sue him for libel (written testimonial or reference) or slander (spoken testimonial or reference) and the defence of justification, i.e. the truth of the statement in that there was a conviction, is a defence to the employer only if he can show that he acted without malice.

(b) **To the former employee**, for libel and slander if there are statements in a testimonial or reference which affect the employee's reputation. However, the situation is one of qualified privilege and the employee would have to prove malice in the employer.

As regards the *ownership* of a written testimonial or reference, this is in the employee to whom it is given and a prospective employer is liable in damages to the employee if having received a reference or testimonial he maliciously destroys or defaces it.

An employee who maliciously defaces his own reference or testimonial commits a criminal offence under the Servants' Characters Act, 1792.

Before leaving the contractual duties of the employer, it should be noted that he has other duties in regard to the health safety and welfare of his employees. These are based mainly on the common law of tort and statutes such as the Health and Safety at Work Act, 1974 and the Factories Act, 1961 and are considered separately in Chapter 5.

Duties of an Employee

The duties of an employee are an amalgam of common law principles and statutory provisions and may be considered under the headings which follow.

To exercise reasonable skill and care

At common law an employee who professes to have a particular skill or skills but proves to be incompetent may be summarily dismissed (see p. 109) and the employer has a defence to an action for unfair dismissal (see p. 87).

Again, at common law employees who have no particular or professional skills must still take reasonable care in the performance of their duties and may be dismissed but only if there is a serious breach of this implied term of the contract.

Both types of employees are, of course, required to indemnify the employer against any loss he has suffered because of the employees' negligence (*Lister* v. *Romford Ice & Cold Storage Co. Ltd*, see p. 18).

Finally, under s 7 of the Health and Safety at Work Act, 1974 employees must take reasonable care of their own and other people's health and safety and co-operate with the employer in the carrying out of his duties under the Act. However, should an employee fail to comply with this provision he is guilty of a criminal offence only since the section does not give rise to civil liability.

To carry out lawful and reasonable instructions

Since failure to carry out instructions often results in dismissal, we shall give fuller consideration to this matter when dealing with summary and unfair dismissal (see pp. 88 and 109).

However, there is an implied term requiring obedience to lawful and reasonable instructions, but this does not extend to illegal acts which an employee is not bound to carry out. Thus in *Gregory* v. *Ford*, [1951] 1 All E.R. 121 an employee was required by his employer to drive a vehicle which was not insured against third party risks as is required by what is now the Road Traffic Act, 1972, but the employee did not know that the vehicle was not insured. The employee, by his negligence, injured a third party who brought an action against the employer and the employee and obtained a judgment against both of them. It was held in the High Court that because the employer had instructed the employee to do an illegal act, i.e. to drive an uninsured vehicle, he must indemnify the employee in respect of any civil claim brought against him. It was also said that an employee cannot be required to do an act if that act is unlawful and if he refuses to do so, he is not in breach of any contractual duty.

The duty of fidelity

There is an implied term in every contract of service that the employee will give faithful service to the employer and certain activities of employees are regarded by the law as breaches of that duty of faithful service.

Thus an employee who copies names and addresses of his employer's customers for use after leaving the employment can be prevented from using the lists.

ROBB v. GREEN, [1895] 2 QB 315: Court of Appeal

Facts

The plaintiff was a dealer in live game and eggs. The major part of his business consisted of procuring the eggs, and the hatching, rearing and sale of game birds. For the purpose of carrying on this business the plaintiff occupied game farms at Liphook in Hampshire, and at Elstead, near Godalming. His customers were numerous and for the most part were country gentlemen and their gamekeepers. The plaintiff kept a list of these customers in his order book. The defendant, who was for three years the plaintiff's manager, copied these names and addresses and after leaving the plaintiff's employ set up a similar business on his own and sent circulars both to the plaintiff's customers and their gamekeepers inviting them to do business with him. The plaintiff asked the Court for damages and an injunction.

Judgment

It was held by the Court of Appeal that although there was no express term in the defendant's contract to restrain him from such activities, it was an implied term of the contract of service that the defendant would observe good faith towards his employer during the existence of the confidential relationship between them. The defendant's conduct was a breach of that contract in respect of which the plaintiff was entitled to damages of £150 and an injunction.

The duty of fidelity does not require the employee to disclose his own breaches of duty.

BELL v. LEVER BROS LTD, [1932] AC 161: House of Lords

Facts

Lever Bros had a controlling interest in the Niger Company. Bell was the chairman, and a person called Snelling was the vice-chairman, of the Niger Company's board. Both directors had service contracts which had some time to run. They became redundant as a result of amalgamations and Lever Bros contracted to pay Bell £30,000 and Snelling £20,000 as compensation. These sums were paid over and then it was discovered that Bell and Snelling had committed breaches of duty during their term of office by making small but secret profits on a cocoa pooling scheme. They could, therefore, have been dismissed without compensation. Lever Bros sought to set aside the payments on the ground of mistake.

Judgment

It was held by the House of Lords that the contract was not void because Lever Bros had got what they bargained for, i.e. the cancellation of two service contracts which, though they might have been terminated, were actually in existence when the cancellation agreement was made. The mistake was as to the quality of the two directors and such mistakes do not avoid contracts.

Comment

The case illustrates that the contract of service is not of utmost good faith. An employee is not bound to disclose his wrongdoing to his employer, so that the silence of the two directors did not amount to a misrepresentation which could assist Lever Bros in the setting aside of the agreement.

There is no implied term which requires disclosure to the employer of misconduct by fellow employees. In this connection the Rehabilitation of Offenders Act, 1974 is relevant since, as we have seen, an employee is not bound to disclose his own spent convictions or those of others — in this case fellow-employees.

The duty of fidelity extends to disclosure to the employer of information obtained during the course of employment which is, or may be, of value to the employer. An employee may be restrained from using such information if he is discovered to have it, and if use has been made of it the employee must account to the employer for any profit made.

INDUSTRIAL DEVELOPMENT CONSULTANTS v. COOLEY, [1972] 2 All E.R. 162: High Court

Facts

The defendant was an architect of considerable distinction and attainment in his own sphere. He was employed as managing director by Industrial Development Consultants who provided construction consultancy services. The Eastern Gas Board were offering a lucrative contract in regard to the building of four depots and IDC was very keen to obtain the business. The defendant was acting for IDC in the matter and the Eastern Gas Board made it clear to the defendant that IDC would not obtain the contract because the officers of the Eastern Gas Board did not like IDC's organisation. The defendant realised that he had a good chance of obtaining the contract for himself and he represented to IDC that he was ill and because IDC thought, as a result of these representations, that the defendant was near to a nervous breakdown, he was allowed to terminate his employment with them on short notice. However, just after his employment with IDC terminated the defendant took steps which resulted in his obtaining the Eastern Gas Board contracts for the four depots for himself. In this case IDC sued the defendant for an account of the profit that he would make on the construction of the four depots.

Judgment

It was held by Roskill, J. that the defendant had acted in breach of duty and must account. The fact that IDC might not have obtained the contract itself was immaterial. 'Therefore it cannot be said that it is anything like certain that the plaintiffs would ever have got this contract ... on the other hand, there was always the possibility of the plaintiffs persuading the Eastern Gas Board to change their minds; and ironically enough, it would have been the defendant's duty to try and persuade them to change their minds. It is a curious position under which he should now say that the plaintiffs suffered no loss because he would never have succeeded in persuading them to change their mind.' (per Roskill, J.)

The duty of fidelity does not apply once the employment has ceased and a former employee cannot be prevented from soliciting the customers of his former employer or doing business with them in the absence of a special provision in the contract of service. However, a former employee may be prevented from using trade secrets or confidential information (see below).

Confidential information

It is also an implied term of a contract of service that the employee will not disclose trade secrets or confidential information acquired during employment. There is no need for an express provision in the contract.

An employee can be restrained from using information or passing it on to another and third parties who receive it can be restrained from using it. However, the employee's knowledge of trade secrets and information must be readily separable and not merely part of the total experience which he has gained from the employment since he cannot be prevented from using what he has honestly and inevitably acquired by experience. The following cases are illustrative of the above principles.

PRINTERS & FINISHERS v. HOLLOWAY (No. 2), [1964] 3 All E.R.
731: High Court

Facts

The plaintiffs brought an action against Holloway, their former works
manager, and others, including Vita-tex Ltd, into whose employment
Holloway had subsequently entered, claiming injunctions against
Holloway and other defendants based, as regards Holloway, on an
alleged breach of an implied term in his contract of service with the
plaintiffs that he should not disclose or make improper use of confidential information relating to the plaintiffs' trade secrets. Holloway's
contract did not contain an express covenant relating to non-disclosure
of trade secrets.

The plaintiffs were flock printers and had built up their own fund of
'know-how' in this field. The action against Vita-tex arose because
Holloway had, on one occasion, taken a Mr James, who was an employee
of Vita-tex Ltd, round the plaintiffs' factory. Mr James's visit took
place in the evening and followed a chance meeting between himself
and Holloway. However, the plant was working and James did see a
number of processes. It also appeared that Holloway had, during his
employment, made copies of certain of the plaintiffs' documentary
material and had taken these copies away with him when he left their
employ. The plaintiffs sought an injunction to prevent the use or disclosure of the material contained in the copies of documents made by
Holloway.

Judgment

It was held by Mr Justice Cross that the plaintiffs were entitled to an
injunction against Holloway so far as the documentary material was
concerned, although there was no express term in his contract regarding non-disclosure of secrets.

However, no injunction would be granted restraining Holloway from
putting at the disposal of Vita-tex Ltd his memory of particular features of the plaintiffs' plant and processes. He was under no express
contract not to do so and the Court would not extend its equitable
jurisdiction to restrain breach of confidence in this instance. Holloway's
knowledge of the plaintiffs' trade secrets was not readily separable from
his general knowledge of flock printing.

In addition, an injunction would be granted restraining Vita-tex Ltd
from making use of the information acquired by Mr James on his visit.

Comment

In addition to obtaining an injunction to stop a third party using the information, it is also possible to sue that third party in damages. (See *Seager* v. *Copydex Ltd*, [1967] 1 WLR 923.)

MORRIS & CO. v. SAXELBY, [1916] 1 A.C. 688: House of Lords

Facts

On leaving school Saxelby entered the drawing office of a company engaged in the manufacture of lifting machinery, pulley blocks and travelling cranes. The company had its head office and works in Loughborough and branch offices in eight large cities. Eventually Saxelby became head of one of the company's departments. He entered into a covenant not to engage in a similar business in the United Kingdom for a period of seven years from the date of leaving the company's service. In this action the company sought to enforce that covenant.

Judgment

It was held by the House of Lords that it was unreasonably wide, having regard to Saxelby's interests, because it would 'deprive him for a lengthened period of employing, in any part of the United Kingdom, that mechanical and technical skill and knowledge which, as I have said, his own industry, observation, and intelligence have enabled him to acquire in the very specialised business of the appellants, thus forcing him to begin life afresh, as it were, and depriving him of the means of supporting himself and his family'. (per Lord Atkinson.)

However, it should be noted that an employee is under no implied obligation not to disclose information concerning his employer's misconduct if it ought in the public interest to be disclosed to a person having a proper interest to receive it.

INITIAL SERVICES v. PUTTERILL, [1967] 3 All E.R. 145: Court of Appeal

Facts

The first defendant was employed by the plaintiff launderers as sales manager but he resigned and took a number of the plaintiffs' documents which he handed to reporters of the *Daily Mail*, who were the second defendants. He also gave the reporters of the same newspaper information about the company's affairs. The newspaper published articles alleging a liaison system between launderers to keep up their prices, and that the plaintiffs had increased their prices after the imposition of the Selective Employment Tax ostensibly to offset that tax when in fact they were, so the paper alleged, getting substantial extra profit. On the plaintiffs' action for breach of an implied term of the defendant's contract of service that he would not disclose to strangers confidential information obtained by him in the course of his employment, the defendant alleged by way of defence that the plaintiffs had agreements which ought to have been registered under the Restrictive Trade Practices Act, 1956 (see now Restrictive Trade Practices Act, 1976), and that they ought to have been referred to the Monopolies Commission. He further alleged that the plaintiffs had issued misleading circulars about their reasons for raising their prices. The plaintiffs brought these proceedings prior to trial in order to strike out the defence.

Judgment

It was held by the Court of Appeal that:

(i) the employee was under no obligation not to disclose information which ought, in the public interest, to be disclosed to a person having a proper interest to receive it;

(ii) it was at least arguable that the information supplied by the defendant was in the above category;

(iii) the allegations in the defence could not be said to be so invalid that they ought to be struck out.

Comment

There was argument on the question as to whether the Press was the proper authority for the receipt of confidential information but the Court did not feel that this doubt was enough to invalidate the defence at this stage.

Inventions by employees

As regards employee inventions made after 1 June 1978, the position in regard to ownership is covered by the Patents Act, 1977 and we shall not consider the law relating to inventions made before that time.

S 39 of the 1977 Act provides that an employee's invention belongs to his employer *if the employer can prove*:

(i) that it was made by the employee in the course of his normal duties; or

(ii) that although it was made outside the course of his normal duties, it was the result of a specific assignment to be given to the employee; or

(iii) that it was made during the course of employment and that employment imposed upon the employee a special obligation to further the interests of the undertaking.

If the employer cannot satisfy the Patent court as to the above matters the invention belongs to the employee even though it was made at his place of employment during working hours and by the use of the employer's facilities.

Since the burden of proof is on the employer, it is of importance to establish normal and other duties in the contract of employment, particularly where the employee is likely to make inventions. Matters such as job title and the description of the job are therefore all-important. In addition, since an invention may be claimed by more than one employee it is advisable to keep records of who does what in a particular process so as to reduce controversy as to whose invention it is.

(iii) (above) is designed mainly for managing and technical directors where it may be difficult to describe duties with any precision, the employment being designed in broad terms to further the interests of the undertaking. In view of (iii) (above) most inventions by directors, at least in the areas of the company's operation, will belong to the company.

S 40 of the 1977 Act allows the Patent Court to award compensation to an employee where it is decided that his invention belongs to the employer, provided that the invention is *of outstanding benefit* to the employer. The employee may apply to the Patent Court for an award and may receive, in the terms of the Act, a 'fair share' of the benefit which the invention brings to the employer. The Court may award a lump sum or periodic payment.

Obviously what is of outstanding benefit and what is a fair share have yet to be worked out by the Patent Court, and at present there is no real information as to how these terms will be interpreted.

Terms in a contract of service which attempt to exclude rights to compensation for the employee *in advance* of his making an invention are unenforceable unless there is a collective agreement between the employer and a trade union to which the employee belongs which provides for compensation. If this is the case the employee's contract may exclude the 1977 Act so that he then relies on the provisions of the collective agreement. However, an employee may by agreement with his employer waive his right to compensation for an invention *after* it is made.

The Act applies only to inventions made by employees who work mainly in the UK, though if they do, patents granted by foreign countries are covered.

Copyright

S 4(2) of the Copyright Act, 1956 provides that if an employee or ex-employee has 'in the course of his employment' produced a literary, musical, or artistic work which is capable of protection by copyright, then, subject to any agreement in the contract of service to the contrary, the first owner of that copyright is the employer.

If work capable of protection by copyright is produced other than in the course of employment then the copyright belongs to the employee, but the employer may nevertheless restrain its publication if it would be a breach of contract, as where the work discloses facts or ideas which can properly be regarded as the property of the employer.

A good illustration of this is provided by *Stevenson, Jordan & Harrison Ltd* v. *Macdonald & Evans*, (1952) (see p. 4).

Bribery and corruption of agents and employees

The civil and criminal law relating to the bribery and corruption of agents and employees, sometimes referred to as the payment of 'slush money' is of increasing importance as standards of honesty decline.

The provisions of United Kingdom civil law

So far as the civil law is concerned, a bribe is the payment of a secret commission by a third party to an agent or employee.

On the assumption, therefore, that X has engaged an agent or employee (AE) to sell X's property to Y for the best price that AE can get, then in order to establish a bribe the following matters must be proved:

(i) that Y made a gift or other consideration to AE;

(ii) that Y made the gift or other consideration knowing that AE was the agent or employee of X;

(iii) that Y failed to disclose to X that he had made the gift or other consideration to AE.

The authority for (i) to (iii) above is the decision of the Court in *Industries and General Mortgage Co.* v. *Lewis*, [1949] 2 All E.R. 573.

Once these matters have been proved then it is presumed:

(a) that Y's motive was corrupt;

(b) that AE was affected and influenced by the payment and did not conduct the transaction in the best interests of his employer. The presumptions in (a) and (b) are conclusive, which means that no evidence is admissible to contradict them.

Consequently, once the receipt of a bribe has been proved the employer is not required to show that AE's mind was in actual fact influenced by the payment of the bribe. Thus in *Shipway* v. *Broadwood*, [1899] 1 Q.B. 369 the defendant wished to buy a pair of horses and asked a veterinary (P) to find him a pair. P suggested that the defendant should buy a pair of horses which were being sold by a Worcester horse dealer. The defendant agreed to buy them if P passed them as sound. P gave the defendant a certificate of soundness and the horses were delivered to the defendant who sent a cheque to the dealer. On delivery the horses were found to be unsound and the defendant returned them and stopped the cheque. The dealer now sued on the cheque and the defence was that there had been a total failure of consideration and that the plaintiff had warranted the horses sound. The plaintiff succeeded when he first appeared before a court, the judge finding that no warranty had been given and that the defendant had simply agreed to buy if P certified the horses sound, as he had done. Evidence showed that P had received a commission from S but the judge gave no ruling as to the effect of this on P's judgment. It was held – by the Court of Appeal – that no such ruling was necessary; it was possible to find for the defendant, which the Court of Appeal did, merely on the evidence that a commission had been paid. It was not necessary to inquire whether P had been biased by receiving it.

In addition, Y is regarded as a party to the breach of duty by AE and X can rescind (or set aside) the transaction which AE entered into with Y on X's behalf. Thus if AE had sold X's land to Y having received a bribe from Y in the process, X would not be required to convey the land to Y, or if he had done so, he could ask the court for an order of rescission, the effect of which would be to require Y to reconvey the land to X. If Y refused to comply with the order of rescission he would be in contempt of court and could be punished by fine or, as a last resort, imprisonment until he had purged his contempt by reconveying the land to X.

In addition to the right to rescind X can also recover the bribe from AE, if he has received it, or from Y if it has been promised but not paid. Furthermore, X can also sue for damages and these are awarded without deduction of the amount of any bribe recovered by X. Thus in *Salford Corporation* v. *Lever*, [1891] 1 Q.B. 168, the defendant was a coal supplier and had at various times supplied coal to the corporation. The negotiations regarding these sales were conducted by the corporation's Gas Manager, Mr Hunter. Evidence showed that Hunter induced Lever to put up the price of his coal by what was then one shilling (5p) per ton, and to pay this over to Hunter by saying that unless Lever agreed to do this he would buy coal for the corporation elsewhere. At the time of the action the excess paid by the corporation to Lever was £2329 and they sought to recover that sum from Lever. Lever's defence was that the corporation had already recovered the money from Hunter. Nevertheless, it was held that Lever was guilty of fraud and his fraud was wholly independent of that of Hunter and therefore both were liable to pay to the corporation the sums obtained by their separate frauds.

Provisions of United Kingdom criminal law

Criminal liability in regard to bribery and corruption of agents and employees is to be found in the common law of conspiracy (see below) and in three Acts of Parliament as follows:

(a) **The Public Bodies Corrupt Practices Act**, 1889. This Act deals with bribery and corruption of or by employees of public bodies. Members of public bodies are also included so that, for example, bribery and corruption of or by councillors of local authorities, is covered.

Any person who is convicted of an offence under the Act may be imprisoned for a period not exceeding two years and/or fined up to a maximum of £500 *for each offence*.

A criminal court may also order repayment of any reward received. There are also provisions relating to disqualification from voting and from being a member of any public body together with possible forfeiture of, e.g., pension rights. The consent of the Attorney General is necessary before proceedings can be taken.

An example of the situation in which the Act of 1889 would apply is where, say, a local authority inspector received a fee for not instituting a prosecution against a dairyman for adulteration of milk.

However, the Act is not confined to local authorities but extends to any body which has public or statutory duties to carry out. Thus in *Director of Public Prosecutions* v. *Holly and Manners*, [1977] 1 All E.R. 316 the House of Lords decided that area gas boards were included and upheld a conviction of an employee of a gas board for receiving, and a third party for giving, a bribe so that a particular contractor would be shown favour in regard to work to be done for the board.

(b) **The Prevention of Corruption Act, 1906.** This Act applies to corruption of and by agents in general. The expression 'agent' includes any person employed by or acting for another. The maximum penalty is a period of imprisonment not exceeding two years and/or a fine of up to £500 for each offence.

The consent of the Attorney General or Solicitor General is required before proceedings can be instituted.

(c) **The Prevention of Corruption Act, 1916.** This Act increases the maximum penalty where an offence under the 1889 and 1906 Acts *relates to a contract or a proposal for a contract with a Government department.* In such a case the maximum period of imprisonment is increased to seven years.

In addition there is a presumption that any payment or gift or other consideration was received corruptly so that a person accused has to bring evidence to show that this was probably not the case. If he cannot, the prosecution will succeed.

The common law of conspiracy, e.g. conspiracy to defraud, is also available in criminal prosecutions for bribery and corruption. This is illustrated by the case of *R.* v. *Tilbrook, Sivalingam*, [1978] Crim. L.R. 172. This case is also a modern example of sentencing policy in corruption cases. In *Tilbrook* the employment of one of the accused, A, required him to invite tenders for printing work. He received corrupt payments from B Ltd for accepting their tenders rather than lower ones from other firms. The other person accused, C, received payments from A and B Ltd for not informing his superiors of what was going on. From 1966 to 1974 when he left to take up other employment, C received about £9000 in bribes. A continued his activities and probably received very much more. A was the dominant figure in the arrangement. C disclosed everything to the authorities, including his own offences, and also gave evidence for the Crown. At the trial C pleaded guilty to eight offences of corruption and A was convicted of conspiracy to defraud and eight offences of corruption. C was sentenced to a total of three years imprisonment in respect of the eight offences. A received five years imprisonment for conspiracy and two years for each of the corruption charges, these to run concurrently, making seven years in all. He was also fined £5000 for conspiracy with a further 12 months imprisonment on failure to pay. The case indicates that the courts take the matter of corruption seriously, particularly when large sums of money are involved.

Agents and employees receiving secret profits or having conflicting interests

A further way in which an agent or employee may act against the interests of the person engaging him is the obtaining of a secret benefit because of his position in the organisation or during the course of negotiating business for the organisation. Where this has taken place the civil law will allow the organisation concerned to recover the value of the secret profit. An example is to be found in *Industrial Development Consultants Ltd* v. *Cooley*, (1972) (see p. 70).

The making of secret profits is not a criminal offence under the Prevention of Corruption legislation referred to in the previous section. However, as regards company directors, failure to disclose an interest in a contract or proposed contract with the company of which they are directors may result in a prosecution leading to a fine not exceeding £100 (s 199, Companies Act, 1948).

Indemnity and contribution

We have already given a general consideration to the duty of an employee to indemnify his employer and to contribute towards payment of damages caused by the employee but for which his employer has been made vicariously liable (see p. 18).

There are one or two points to add here, the first of which is that the employee does not need to indemnify his employer if he injures a third person in the course of doing work, under the direction of his employer, which he does not normally do.

Thus in *Harvey* v. *R.G. O'Dell Ltd*, [1958] 2 Q.B. 78, the defendants sent Harvey and another man, X, out on a job which was to last all day. They went for their lunch to the nearest town which was Maidenhead and in order to get there X had to use his motor cycle which the Court said, in the circumstances, the two men had at least an implied permission from the employer to use. While they were returning X's negligent driving caused the death of Harvey, and McNair, J. said that the defendants were liable because the men were within the scope of their employment. However, he also said, distinguishing *Lister* v. *Romford Ice & Cold Storage Co. Ltd*, (1957) (see p. 18) that since X was employed as a storekeeper and not as the driver of a motor cycle, he need not indemnify the employer because, although he drove negligently, he was not in breach of his contract as a storekeeper.

As regards contribution, since under the doctrine of vicarious liability employer and employee are regarded as joint tortfeasors, an employer who pays the damages awarded in regard to an injury caused by his employee's negligence is entitled to a contribution from the employee under the Law Reform (Married Women and Tortfeasors) Act, 1935. This may amount to a full indemnity as in *Ryan* v. *Fildes*, [1938] 3 All E.R. 517 where the managers of a school were held entitled to a full indemnity from a school mistress who had injured a schoolboy.

However, as we have seen, there will be no full indemnity but only a contribution if the employer has been negligent himself and so contributed to the damage as where, e.g., he has given certain work to an employee who lacks experience of it (see *Jones* v. *Manchester Corporation*, (1952) (see p. 19).

3 Contract of Employment—Termination

UNFAIR DISMISSAL — GENERALLY

Before a person can ask an industrial tribunal to consider a claim that another has unfairly dismissed him it is once again essential to establish that the relationship of employer and employee exists between them.

Some consideration has already been given to this on pp. 1-6 in terms of the control test, organisation test and the concept of the independent contractor, and from this we know that the terminology used by the parties is not conclusive (see *Ferguson* v. *John Dawson & Partners (Contractors)*, (1976), p. 6).

However, we deal here more particularly with cases before industrial tribunals which have been interpeting what is now s. 153 of the EPCA. This provides that an employee is a person who works under a contract of service or apprenticeship, written, oral, express or implied.

An example of a case where a person failed in an unfair dismissal claim because he was unable to show that he was an employee is given below.

MASSEY v. CROWN LIFE INSURANCE CO., [1978] 2 All E.R. 576: Court of Appeal

Facts

Mr Massey was employed by Crown Life as the manager of their Ilford branch from 1971 to 1973, the company paying him wages and deducting tax. In 1973 on the advice of his accountant Mr Massey registered a business name of J.L. Massey and Associates and with that new name entered into an agreement with Crown Life under which he carried out the same duties as before as a self-employed person. The Inland Revenue were content that he should change to being taxed under Schedule D as a self-employed person. His employment was terminated and he claimed to have been unfairly dismissed.

Judgment

The Court of Appeal held that being self-employed he could not be unfairly dismissed. Lord Justice Lawton said that to allow a man to claim that he was self-employed in order to claim tax advantages and also to deny that he was self-employed in order to claim compensation for unfair dismissal strained the highly desirable union between fairness, commonsense and the law almost to breaking point. In addition Lord Denning said: 'In the present case there is a perfectly genuine agreement entered into at the instance of Mr Massey on the footing that he is "self-employed". He gets the benefit of it by avoiding tax deductions and getting his pension contributions returned. I do not see that he can come along afterwards and say it is something else in order to claim that he has been unfairly dismissed. Having made his bed as being "self-employed" he must lie on it. He is not under a contract of service.'

In addition to showing that he is an employee the claimant must comply with an *age requirement*. The unfair dismissal provisions do not, under s 64 of the EPCA, apply to the dismissal of an employee from any employment if the employee has on or before the effective date of termination attained the age which, in the undertaking in which he was employed, was the normal retiring age for an employee holding the position which he held, or, if a man, attained the age of 65, or, if a woman, attained the age of 60.

The decision of the House of Lords in *Nothman* v. *London Borough of Barnet*, [1979] 1 All E.R. 142 is important here. In that case the House of Lords decided that a woman teacher who, at 61, had not reached the normal retiring age for her profession of 65 was not deprived by the EPCA s 64 provision of her right not to be unfairly dismissed. The House of Lords held that the provision in the second part of the section, that a man had to be under 65 and a woman under 60, did not apply. These ages should be read as applying only in cases where there was no normal retiring age. In consequence the House of Lords decided that an industrial tribunal had jurisdiction to hear Miss Nothman's complaint of unfair dismissal against her employers, the London Borough of Barnet.

As regards the period of employment, s 64 of the EPCA (as amended) provides that the unfair dismissal provisions do not apply to the dismissal of an employee from any employment if the employee was not continuously employed for a period of not less than 52 weeks ending with the effective date of termination. In addition, s 3 of the EPCA states that no account shall be taken of employment during any period when the hours of employment are normally less than 16 hours weekly.

If the hours are normally 16 per week it does not matter that in a particular week or weeks the employee actually works less than 16 hours. Such a week will count if for the whole or part of the week there is a contract which normally involves working 16 or more hours. Furthermore, if the contract does not require the employee to work 16 hours per week but because of voluntary overtime he does in fact work 16 or more hours, then those weeks will count even though some of the work is voluntary overtime.

In addition, it should be noted that an employee who is not given adequate time to complete his work during working hours so that some has to be taken home may regard the additional work at home as contractual working time for the purpose of the 16-hours rule.

The decision of the Employment Appeal Tribunal in *Lake* v. *Essex County Council*, [1978] I.R.L.R. 24 is of importance here. The case was brought at a time when the present 16-hour rule was a 21-hour rule but, that apart, is applicable today. In the case the EAT held that work done by a teacher in her spare time outside school hours, such as marking or preparation work, which was reasonably necessary for her job, should be included in computing the number of hours for which she was employed in order to see whether she had worked sufficient hours to enable her to bring a complaint of unfair dismissal. The local authority allocated three hours, 40 minutes per week out of 19 hours, 25 minutes for preparation and marking but the Court accepted that this was not sufficient and Mrs Lake had to do additional work at home. In consequence she was entitled to complain of unfair dismissal.

As regards persons ordinarily employed outside Great Britain, s 141 of the EPCA states that an employee has no protection against unfair dismissal if he is engaged in work wholly or mainly outside Great Britain.

The true test appears to be where the employee is *based* and not how often he is abroad. Thus in *Wilson* v. *Maynard Shipbuilding Consultants*, [1978] 2 All E.R. 78 – Court of Appeal, a management consultant who resided in Great Britain was paid here and had the use of an office here. The Court of Appeal decided that he was eligible to complain of unfair dismissal, although during the period July 1973 to September 1975 he spent 50 weeks in Italy and 40 weeks in the UK. Lord Justice Megaw summed up the position in his judgment when he said: 'In such a case as the present it appears to us that the correct approach is to look at the terms of the contract, express and implied . . . in order to ascertain where, looking at the whole period contemplated by the contract, the employee's base is to be. It is, in the absence of special factors leading to a contrary conclusion, the country where his base is to be which is likely to be the place where he is to be treated as ordinarily working under his contract of employment. Where his base, under the contract, is to be will depend on the examination of all relevant contract terms. These will be likely to include any such terms as expressly define his headquarters, or which indicate where the travels involved in his employment begin and end; where his private residence, his home, is, or is expected to be; where, and perhaps in what currency, he is to be paid; whether he is to be required to pay National Insurance contributions in Great Britain. These are merely examples of factors which, among many others that may be found to exist in individual cases, may be relevant in deciding where the employee's base is for the purpose of his work, looking to the whole normal, anticipated duration of the employment.'

DISMISSAL — MEANING OF

An employee cannot claim unfair dismissal unless there has first been a dismissal recognised by law. The matter may be considered under the headings set out below.

Actual Dismissal

This does not normally give rise to problems since most employees would recognise the words of an actual dismissal, whether given orally or in writing.

However, sometimes there may be a dismissal in a fit of temper which the employer afterwards tries to withdraw by an effort to reinstate the employee. Nevertheless, an employee may show (and the burden of proof is on him) that he was dismissed provided that the words used carried that import and were not mere abuse. Thus in *Chesham Shipping* v. *Rowe*, [1977] I.R.L.R. 391, Employment Appeal Tribunal, Captain Rowe's employer summarily dismissed him in a fit of temper but, after calming down and realising that Captain Rowe was not to blame reinstated Captain Rowe. It was held by the EAT that the Industrial Tribunal were entitled to find that Captain Rowe had been dismissed and had not agreed to be reinstated. Although Captain Rowe's employer was in a blazing temper, he had indicated an intention to dismiss. The EAT also decided that reinstatement cannot be achieved unilaterally, the employee must also agree to be reinstated. In consequence Chesham Shipping's appeal against a finding of unfair dismissal was dismissed.

Constructive Dismissal

This occurs where it is the employee who leaves his job but he is compelled to do so by the conduct of his employer. The employer's conduct may be such a fundamental breach as to be regarded as a repudiation of a contract but it may also be mere unreasonable conduct which could not be regarded as a fundamental or repudiatory breach. Illustrative cases appear below.

WESTERN EXCAVATING LTD v. SHARP, [1978] 1 All E.R. 713: Court of Appeal

Facts

Under the terms of his employment if Mr Sharp worked extra time he could have time off in lieu. In February 1976 he asked for three hours off to play cards for a team. He was told that he could not have the time off that afternoon as there was too much work; nevertheless he went to play cards. The next day he was dismissed. The disciplinary panel set up by the employers substituted five days' suspension without pay for the dismissal. That left Mr Sharp in financial difficulties and he asked his employer for an advance on his accrued holiday pay. This was refused, as was a request for a loan of £40, and he then left his employment in order to obtain his holiday pay and brought a claim for unfair dismissal. That claim was upheld by an industrial tribunal and the Employment Appeal Tribunal and the matter came before the Court of Appeal.

Judgment

The Court of Appeal decided that in order to establish constructive dismissal it must be shown that the employer was guilty of conduct which was sufficiently serious to amount to a breach of the contract of service. If it was, then the employee could be regarded as unfairly dismissed even though it was the employee who left the employment. The other approach which had been adopted in cases before tribunals, i.e. that if the employer acted 'unreasonably' an employee might leave and yet be regarded as having been unfairly dismissed, was wrong.

'The present case is a good illustration of a 'whimsical decision'. Applying the test of 'unreasonable conduct', the Industrial Tribunal decided by a majority of two to one in favour of the man. The Employment Appeal Tribunal would, all three of them, have decided in favour of the employer, but felt that it was a matter of fact on which they could not reverse the Industrial Tribunal. So, counting heads, it was four to two in favour of the employers, but yet the case was decided against them, because of the test of 'unreasonable conduct'.

'If the 'contract test' had been applied, the result would have been plain. There was no dismissal, constructive or otherwise, by the company. The company were not in breach at all. Nor had they repudiated the contract at all. Mr Sharp left of his own accord without anything wrong done by the company. His claim should have been rejected. The decision against the company was most unjust to them. I would allow the appeal accordingly.' (per Lord Denning, MR.)

Comment

In spite of the decision of the Court of Appeal that unreasonable conduct in the employer was not enough, there have been cases since *Sharp* where the court has decided that unreasonable conduct may be enough to amount to a repudiatory dismissal. Thus in *Palmanor* v. *Cedron*, [1978] I.C.R. 1008, EAT, an employee barman was held to have been constructively dismissed when he left because the manager swore at him. Again in *Robinson* v. *Crompton Parkinson*, [1978] I.C.R. 401, EAT, an employee of good character was falsely accused of theft and the police were called and he eventually resigned after being promised a written apology which he did not get. He applied for compensation for unfair dismissal, but the Industrial Tribunal held that he had not proved that the employer's action was such as to bring the contract of employment to an end. On appeal to the EAT it was held that the situation did amount to repudiation of the contract of employment, though they sent the case to another Industrial Tribunal for rehearing in case the employer could show some background knowledge to justify his suspicion of the employee. If there had been reasonable grounds for the allegations, however false, the employer may not have appeared quite so unreasonable.

As regards *repudiation*, is failure by an employer to provide work a repudiatory breach under the contract test of Lord Denning? We have already considered the view of the common law in this matter (see p. 60), and have seen that in broad terms the position at common law is that the employer has no duty to provide work, so that if he continues to pay wages or salary the employee cannot regard the employer as in breach of contract and has no right of action for wrongful dismissal but must merely accept his pay.

However, in cases of unfair dismissal before industrial tribunals there has been a tendency to imply a duty to provide work as a term in the contract of service. Thus in *Bosworth* v. *Angus Jowett & Co.*, [1977] I.R.L.R. 374, B was employed as a sales director under a fixed term contract expiring on 31 May 1977. However, on 20 January 1977 he was told that he would not be required to work out the term of his contract and he was also barred from Jowett's premises, though he was paid in full to 31 May 1977. An Industrial Tribunal held that Jowett had repudiated B's contract of employment by withdrawing permission for him to continue to carry out his duties. He had agreed in his contract to give his whole time to such duties as the board of directors might from time to time assign to him, and the contract also provided for a bonus scheme which was based on their profits so that B could not participate in these after Jowett had withdrawn his right to work. Furthermore, the Industrial Tribunal held that B's reputation in the trade could be damaged if it became known that Jowett had refused to let him complete his contract. Consequently B had been constructively dismissed and the fact that he had accepted his salary until 31 May 1977 did not affect that position because repudiation can terminate a contract of employment whether that repudiation is accepted by the injured party or not.

Finally, although constructive dismissal usually involves some act or acts of unfairness by the employer towards the employee, a constructive dismissal may in some circumstances be fair. Thus in *Industrial Rubber Products* v. *Gillon*, [1977] I.R.L;R. 389 G's pay was increased by Industrial but then Industrial discovered that they were inadvertently in breach of the Government's non-statutory pay policy. Accordingly they reduced all rates of pay including G's and G resigned. It was held by an Industrial Tribunal on the issue of the unfair dismissal of G that to cause a person to leave by reducing his pay could be a form of constructive dismissal but in this case the dismissal was fair since Industrial had at least a moral, though not a legal, duty to comply with the Government's pay policy.

Fixed Term Contracts

When a fixed term contract expires and is not renewed there is a dismissal. However, where the contract is for two years or more the employee may have waived his right to complain of unfair dismissal (see further p. 97).

Dismissal, grounds for

If an employer is to escape liability for unfair dismissal he must under s 57 of the EPCA show that he acted *reasonably*, and indeed under s 53 of the EPCA the employer is required to give his reasons for dismissal to the employee in writing.

It should be remembered that the question whether a dismissal is fair or not is a matter of *fact* for the particular tribunal hearing the case and one cannot predict with absolute accuracy what a particular tribunal will do on the facts of a particular case. Basically, when all is said and done, and every legal nuance has been considered the ultimate question for a tribunal is 'was the dismissal fair and reasonable' in fact.

(a) **Reasons justifying dismissal.** These are as follows:
(i) *lack of capability*. This would usually arise at the beginning of employment where it becomes clear at an early stage that the employee cannot do the job in terms of lack of skill or mental or physical health. It should be borne in mind that the longer a person is in employment, the more difficult it is to establish lack of capability.

By way of illustration we may, perhaps, consider some cases which have been decided on this matter before industrial tribunals, provided we bear in mind that they are examples only and by no means exhaustive of all the possibilities.

For example, in *Alidair* v. *Taylor*, [1977] I.C.R. 446 — Employment Appeal Tribunal, the pilot of an aircraft had made a faulty landing which damaged the aircraft. There was a Board of Inquiry which found that the faulty landing was caused by a lack of flying knowledge on the part of the pilot who was dismissed from his employment. It was held that the employee had not been unfairly dismissed, the Tribunal taking the view that where, as in this case, one failure to reach a high degree of skill could have serious consequences, an instant dismissal could be justified.

Again, in *Coward* v. *John Menzies (Holdings)*, [1977] I.R.L.R. 428 — Employment Appeal Tribunal, JM proposed to move C, a hardworking and conscientious branch manager, to Swansea as assistant manager for re-training, on the same salary. This action was taken because JM felt that C lacked certain managerial qualities and it was accepted that if the re-training had been successful he would probably been re-promoted to manager. However, C refused to accept the proposal and was dismissed, and it was held by the Tribunal that the dismissal was fair. The case illustrates that if an employer believes that there is a degree of incapability in an employee and offers to put that right by re-training, then an employee who refuses such an offer will in general terms be unable to claim unfair dismissal where that follows upon his refusal to accept re-training.

(ii) *Conduct*. This is always a difficult matter to deal with and much will depend upon the circumstances of the case. However, incompetence and neglect are relevant, as are disobedience and misconduct, e.g. by assaulting fellow employees. Immorality and habitual drunkenness could also be brought under this heading and, so it seems, can dress, where this can be shown to affect adversely the way in which the contract of service is performed.

BOYCHUK v. H.J. SYMONS HOLDINGS LTD, [1977] I.R.L.R. 375: Employment Appeal Tribunal

Facts

Miss B was employed by S Ltd as an accounts audit clerk but her duties involved contact with the public from time to time. Miss B insisted on wearing badges which proclaimed the fact that she was a lesbian and from May 1976 she wore one or other of the following:

(i) a lesbian symbol consisting of two circles with crosses (indicating women) joined together;

(ii) badges with the legends 'Gays Against Fascism' and 'Gay Power';

(iii) a badge with the legend 'Gay Switchboard' with a telephone number on it and the words 'Information Service for Homosexual Men and Women';

(iv) a badge with the word 'Dyke' on it, indicating to the initiated that she was a lesbian.

These were eventually superseded by a white badge with the words 'Lesbians Ignite' written in large letters on it. Nothing much had happened in regard to the wearing of the earlier badges but when she began wearing the 'Lesbians Ignite' badge there were discussions about it between her and her employers. She was told she must remove it — which she was not willing to do — and if she did not she would be dismissed. She would not remove the badge and was dismissed on 16 August 1976, and then made a claim for compensation for unfair dismissal.

No complaint was made regarding the manner of her dismissal in terms, e.g. of proper warning. The straight question was whether her employers were entitled to dismiss her because she insisted on wearing the badge. An Industrial Tribunal had held that in all the circumstances the dismissal was fair because it was within an employer's discretion to instruct an employee not to wear a particular sign or symbol which could cause offence to customers and fellow-employees. Miss B appealed to the Employment Appeal Tribunal.

Judgment

The Employment Appeal Tribunal dismissed her appeal and affirmed that her dismissal was fair. The judgment of the Court was read by Mr Justice Phillips who made the following points:

(i) There was no question of Miss B having been dismissed because she was a lesbian or because of anything to do with her private life or private behaviour. Such a case would be entirely different and raise different questions. This was only a case where she had been dismissed because of her conduct at work — that, the judge said, must be clearly understood;

(ii) The decision did not mean that an employer by a foolish or unreasonable judgment of what could be expected to be offensive could impose some unreasonable restriction on an employee. However, the decision did mean that a reasonable employer, who was after all ultimately responsible for the interests of the business, could be allowed to decide what upon reflection or mature consideration could be offensive to customers and fellow-employees, and he need not wait to see whether the business will in fact be damaged before he takes steps in the matter.

POEL—7 ••

(iii) *Redundancy*. Where a person is redundant, his employer cannot be expected to continue the employment, although there are safeguards in the matter of unfair selection for redundancy (see p. 91).

(iv) *Failure to join a trade union*. Where there is a union membership agreement, e.g. for a closed shop, it is fair to dismiss an employee who will not join or threatens to resign from an appropriate union, except where his reasons for doing so are based on religious beliefs. We have already considered the case of *Saggers* v. *British Railways Board*, (1977) (see p. 63) where the Employment Appeal Tribunal said that in considering whether an employee's refusal to join a trade union was because of a genuine objection on the grounds of religious belief, an Industrial Tribunal should have regard not only to the general creed of the religious sect to which the employee belongs but also to his own personal beliefs.

(v) *Other grounds*. An employer may on a wide variety of grounds which are not specified by any legislation satisfy an industrial tribunal that a dismissal was fair and reasonable.

Thus in *Ahmad* v. *Inner London Education Authority*, [1977] I.C.R. 49 – Court of Appeal, A, a teacher and devout Muslim, took time off on Friday for religious purposes and refused to accept the Authority's offer to employ him on the basis of a four-and-a-half-day week. He then left and claimed a constructive unfair dismissal. The Court of Appeal held that the dismissal was not unfair by English law and incidentally decided that there was no infringement of Art. 9 of the European Convention on Human Rights.

Crime and suspicion of crime may also be brought under this head, though if dismissal is based upon suspicion of crime the suspicion must be reasonable and in all cases the employee must be told that dismissal is contemplated and in the light of this information be allowed to give explanations and make representations against dismissal. Thus in *Lees* v. *The Orchard*, [1978] I.R.L.R. 20 – Employment Appeal Tribunal, an employer put a till roll into a cash register in October 1976 when the honesty of one employee, a shop assistant, was in question. In January 1977 the shop assistant was seen, it was alleged, to enter a transaction into a book without putting any money into the till. The shop assistant was dismissed the following day because no entry was found on the till roll. An Industrial Tribunal found that the dismissal was fair and the shop assistant appealed to the EAT. Her appeal was allowed on the basis that the Tribunal had erred when they found the dismissal fair. If an employer wants to justify dismissal for suspected dishonesty he must show reasonable grounds for those suspicions. In this case there were a number of ways in which the money could have gone missing without dishonesty on the shop assistant's part. Furthermore, since the evidence was doubtful as to what happened when the shop assistant was confronted with the alleged dishonesty prior to dismissal, the Tribunal was wrong to find that she had been given a reasonable opportunity to explain her position.

Furthermore, a dismissal is fair if to continue the employment would be contrary to law. Thus the dismissal of a lorry driver would, on general principles, be fair if he lost his licence. However, the mere fact that an employment has become illegal is not *conclusive* evidence that a particular dismissal is reasonable. Thus in *Sutcliffe & Eaton* v. *Pinney*, [1977] I.R.L.R. 349 – Employment Appeal Tribunal, the employee was a trainee hearing aid dispenser learning in what circumstances to advise people to have hearing aids. He was dismissed by his employers because he failed the Hearing Aid Council Examination within the permitted five-year period, and his name was removed from the Register of Hearing Aid Dispensers. The employers alleged that it was a fair dismissal since it is an offence under the Hearing Aid Council Act, 1968 for registered employers to employ unregistered persons. An Industrial Tribunal found that the dismissal was unfair and the employers appealed to the EAT, where it was held that the fact that continuation of a person's employment could result in a breach of an Act of Parliament was not conclusive that the dismissal was reasonable. The Tribunal was entitled to find as it had that if the employers had continued the employment and applied for an extension of the employee's training period there was very little chance that proceedings would be brought against them under the 1968 Act. In these circumstances the employee had been unfairly dismissed.

(b) **Unacceptable reasons for dismissal.** These are as follows:

(i) *Trade union membership.* The dismissal of an employee, regardless of his length of service, because he is a member of or intends to join a trade union, or has taken or proposes to take part in its activities, or because he has refused to join a trade union on the grounds of religious belief, is unfair.

(ii) *Unfair selection for redundancy.* An employee dismissed for redundancy may complain that he has been unfairly dismissed if he is of the opinion that he has been unfairly selected for redundancy, as where the employer has selected him because he is a member of a trade union or takes part in trade union activities, or where the employer has disregarded redundancy selection arrangements, e.g. 'last in, first out'. Ideally, all employers should have proper redundancy agreements on the lines set out in the Department of Employment booklet *Dealing with Redundancies*.

However, even though there is in existence an agreed redundancy procedure, the employer may defend himself by showing a 'special reason' for departing from that procedure, e.g. because the person selected for redundancy lacks the skill and versatility of a junior employee who is retained.

(iii) *Strikes.* If an employee is dismissed during a strike, an industrial tribunal has no power to hear an application for unfair dismissal by that person and in consequence the question as to whether the dismissal is fair or unfair never arises. However, a tribunal can hear a claim in regard to a dismissal during a strike where other employees involved in the strike were not dismissed or, if they were dismissed, were afterwards offered re-engagement by the employer whereas the claimant was not.

(iv) *Dismissal of pregnant employee.* A woman who is dismissed because she is pregnant will be treated as having been unfairly dismissed unless certain circumstances apply, e.g. that she is unable to do her job and cannot be offered, or has refused suitable alternative work. Even in these cases where the dismissal would be regarded as fair, the woman is nevertheless entitled to Maternity Pay and may claim reinstatement after confinement.

In this connection we should consider the decision in *Elegbede* v. *The Wellcome Foundation Ltd*, [1977] I.R.L.R. 383, where the employee, a pensions assistant in a sedentary job, was dismissed by a letter dated 17 February 1977, having been unfit for work since 4 January 1977, owing to hypertension which had been brought on by her pregnancy. An Industrial Tribunal held that she had been unfairly dismissed, saying that her dismissal was, in effect, because she had hypertension not because she was pregnant, since it appeared that a healthy pregnant woman could have done the job. Thus the dismissal, although connected with the pregnancy, was not on the grounds of pregnancy and so it would have been no defence for the employer to show that she could not have been offered alternative work or that she had refused alternative work.

(v) *Pressure on employer to dismiss unfairly.* It is no defence for an employer to say that pressure was put upon him to dismiss an employee unfairly. Thus, if other workers put pressure on an employer to dismiss a non-union member so as, for example, to achieve a closed shop, the employer will have no defence to a claim for compensation for the dismissal if he yields to that pressure.

UNFAIR DISMISSAL AND FRUSTRATION OF THE CONTRACT OF EMPLOYMENT

In cases appearing before industrial tribunals there is a certain interplay between the common law rules of frustration of contract and the statutory provisions relating to unfair dismissal. At common law a contract of service is frustrated by incapacity, e.g. sickness, if that incapacity makes the contract substantially impossible of performance at a particularly vital time. If the contract has been so frustrated then a complaint of unfair dismissal is not available because the contract has been discharged on other grounds, i.e. frustration. Thus termination of a contract of service by frustration is a special area and the rules may be considered under two main headings as follows:

(a) **Key workers.** The more important the job the more likely it is that a court or tribunal will conclude that the contract of service has been frustrated by incapacity, even for a short period.

POUSSARD v. SPIERS & POND, (1876) 1 Q.B.D. 410: Queens Bench Division

Facts

Madame Poussard had entered into an agreement to play a part in an opera, the first performance to take place on 28 November 1874. On 23 November Madame Poussard was taken ill and was unable to appear until 4 December. The defendants had hired a substitute, and discovered that the only way in which they could secure a substitute to take Madame Poussard's place was to offer that person a complete engagement. This they had done, and they refused the services of Madame Poussard when she presented herself on 4 December. The plaintiff now sued for breach of contract.

Judgment

It was held that the failure of Madame Poussard to perform the contract as from the first night was a breach of condition, and the defendants were within their rights in regarding the contract as discharged. In addition, the contract was also frustrated even though the period of absence was short.

Comment

An industrial tribunal will normally take a similar view in regard to a claim for unfair dismissal. Thus in *Hart* v. *A.R. Marshall & Sons (Bulwell)*, [1977] I.C.R. 539, the employee had contracted an industrial disease and in consequence was away from work for 21 months, though he sent medical certificates to his employers on a regular basis. The employee was a night service fitter and regarded as a key worker, and after he had been absent for some five months his employers engaged another person in his place. However, the employers did not give notice to the employee of his dismissal and the employee recovered and returned to work when he was told that there was nothing for him to do. He was given his P.45 form and accrued holiday pay. It appeared that there was no formal written contract of employment or other express provisions for dismissal by reason of illness. An industrial tribunal found that the employee's contract had been brought to an end by frustration so that there was no unfair dismissal and the employee appealed to the Employment Appeal Tribunal. His appeal was dismissed, the EAT agreeing that the contract had been frustrated and that it was reasonable of the employers to replace such a key employee fairly quickly. In addition, the employer's acts during the illness did not amount to recognition of continuance of the contract of employment (see below).

(b) **Other cases.** In cases not involving key workers, the following matters are relevant.

(i) *Terms of the contract.* If a contract has a provision dealing with termination of the contract on incapacity, that provision applies. It is obviously better for both employer and employee to deal with this matter in the contract rather than rely on the somewhat vague position under the general law. A suitable contract term might be as follows:

'Where Mr Bloggs is at any time prevented by illness or accident or other incapacity from properly performing his duties under this agreement, he shall, if required, furnish to the company evidence satisfactory to the company of such incapacity and shall be entitled to receive his full salary for the first three months and one half of his full salary for the next consecutive period of three months during which the incapacity shall continue. If Mr Bloggs shall remain so incapacitated for a longer period than six months in any period of 12 consecutive months, the company shall be entitled forthwith to determine the engagement of Mr Bloggs by notice in writing and thereupon Mr Bloggs shall not be entitled to claim any compensation from the company in respect of such determination.'

(ii) *Period of sick pay.* The contract is unlikely to be frustrated if the employee returns to work during the period for which he is entitled to receive sick pay.

(iii) *Period of sickness.* There are no hard and fast rules by which to determine how long a period of sickness is required before the contract is regarded as frustrated. Each case depends upon its own facts.

STOREY v. FULHAM STEEL WORKS, (1907) 24 T.L.R. 89: Court of Appeal

Facts

The plaintiff was employed by the defendants as manager for a period of five years. After he had been working for two years he became ill and had to have special treatment and a period of convalescence. Six months later he was recovered, but in the meantime the defendants had terminated his employment. The plaintiff now sued for breach of contract at common law and the defendants pleaded that the plaintiff's period of ill-health operated to discharge the contract.

Judgment

It was held that the plaintiff's illness and absence from duty did not go to the root of the contract, and was not so serious as to allow the termination of the agreement.

Comment

As regards industrial tribunals, again the period of absence is a matter of fact and no hard and fast rules can be laid down. Thus in *Spencer* v. *Paragon Wallpapers*, [1977] I.C.R. 301 – Employment Appeal Tribunal the company received an unexpected rush of orders but the employee was absent and his doctor had advised that he should take another six weeks' rest. The employers dismissed him and it was held by the EAT that the employers had acted reasonably in regard to the dismissal on the facts of this case, although there was no general rule as to the length of absence which would justify a dismissal.

(iv) *Nature of illness*. Where the illness is likely to persist or permanently incapacitate the employee, as in the case of a skin disease, then the contract may be regarded as frustrated, though in such a case the employee may be entitled to industrial injuries benefits if the disease was contracted at work.

(v) *Period of employment*. As a general rule, the longer a person has been employed the longer the absence he will be allowed before frustration of the contract occurs.

(vi) *Evidence*. Since, as we have seen, the matter of frustration and the contract of service depends upon the view which the court or tribunal takes of the facts of the case, the matter will in most cases be decided on the evidence which the court or tribunal receives. So far as absence through sickness is concerned the following matters are important:

(a) *Evidence that the contract continues during absence*.

If the employee sends medical certificates regularly and these are accepted by the employer who takes no steps to appoint a full-time replacement and also keeps close contact with the employee, then in general terms this will be good evidence that the contract is not frustrated.

(b) *Evidence that the contract has not continued during absence*.

Where the employer appoints a full-time replacement during the employee's absence this is evidence that the employer, at least, regards the contract as terminated. It is advisable, however, for an employer to attempt to obtain temporary replacements and the case for frustration of the contract is strengthened if the employer can show that efforts were made to obtain temporaries without success so that a full-time replacement was essential if the work was to continue.

Remedies for Unfair Dismissal

Employees may make a complaint of unfair dismissal to an industrial tribunal at any time from the date on which they receive notice until three months after the date of dismissal.

(a) **Conciliation.** An industrial tribunal will not hear a complaint until a conciliation officer has had a chance to see whether he can help. A copy of the complaint made to the industrial tribunal is sent to the conciliation officer, and if he is unable to settle the complaint, nothing said by employer or employee during the process of conciliation will be admissible in evidence before the tribunal.

(b) **Hearing by tribunal.** Where an industrial tribunal hears the case the procedure is in broad terms as follows:

(i) it must be established that the employee has been dismissed and is eligible to complain, e.g. on the grounds of continuous service;

(ii) the employer must then attempt to justify the reason for dismissal, i.e. that the circumstances were reasonable, and the way in which it was done was reasonable.

(c) **Remedies.** If a complaint of unfair dismissal is upheld there are the following possibilities:

(i) *reinstatement or re-engagement*: the employee must be told of his right to reinstatement or re-engagement and asked whether he wishes such an order to be made. If he does, the tribunal must consider whether it would be practical and reasonable in all the circumstances to make such an order. If such an order is made, the employer who does not comply with it when it is practical for him to do so, may find that the tribunal will increase the amount of compensation payable by an amount equal to between 13 and 26 weeks of the employee's pay, or where the dismissal was for an inadmissible reason, such as trade union activities, to between 26 and 52 weeks' pay. There is a statutory maximum amount for one week's pay, i.e. £100, so that the additional award for failure to reinstate or re-engage could be as much as £5,200.

(ii) *Compensation*: A tribunal may make money awards. These are referred to as basic awards and compensatory awards. The basic award is calculated according to the formula for redundancy payments, i.e. for each year of service up to a maximum of 20 years a number of weeks' pay up to a maximum of £100 per week as follows:

Ages 41-65 (60 women) 1½ weeks' pay
Ages 22-40 1 week's pay
Ages 15 to 20 one-half a week's pay

There is a maximum payment of £3000 and a minimum of two weeks' pay.

There may also be a compensatory award based on financial loss as a result of dismissal, the maximum compensatory award being £5750.

(iii) *Dismissal for union membership or activities*: an employee who is of the opinion that he has been unfairly dismissed for a reason connected with his trade union membership or activities may, if he wishes, apply to an industrial tribunal for an order for reinstatement or re-engagement on an interim basis, or for his contract of employment to be revised, until a decision has been made on his complaint. The application must be made within seven days of dismissal, and has to be supported by a signed certificate from an official of the relevant trade union.

Legislation also provides that the amount of a basic award is to be reduced where the dismissal was to some extent caused or contributed to by some action of the employee. In an appropriate case contributory fault may result in a nil award, though this is exceptional. Thus in *Maris* v. *Rotherham Corporation*, [1974] 2 All E.R. 776, which was a case on a similar provision in the Industrial Relations Act of 1971, the employee was convicted of fraud in connection with his employment but was reinstated by the Corporation because they thought that his fellow-employees would not object to this course of conduct. However, there were objections by other employees and they threatened industrial action if the reinstatement continued. Following this, the Corporation dismissed the employee. An Industrial Tribunal reached the conclusion that the employee was unfairly dismissed since the Corporation could not plead the threat of industrial action (which is still the position). However, no compensation was awarded to the employee on the basis of contributory fault.

Avoiding Claims for Unfair Dismissal

It is impossible in a book of this nature to give an exhaustive treatment of this subject. However, some of the major areas of claim avoidance are as follows.

(i) **Fixed-term contracts.** S 142 of the EPCA provides that a claim for unfair dismissal does not apply to dismissal from employment under a contract for a fixed term of two years or more, where the dismissal consists only of the expiry of that term without it being renewed, if before the term so expires the employee has agreed in writing to exclude any claim in respect of rights in relation to unfair dismissal.

If, therefore, the contract is for an appropriate fixed term and is in writing containing a clause under which the employee waives his right to claim for unfair dismissal, then that waiver will eliminate his right to complain if the contract is not renewed at the end of the fixed term. However, the employee must be acting freely and voluntarily when he makes the contract excluding his rights and it should be pointed out to him when he makes the contract that this is the position.

(ii) **Employees on probation.** In general terms an employee cannot complain of unfair dismissal unless he has completed 52 weeks' service of not less than 16 hours per week. Thus a dismissal during that period cannot be the subject of a claim.

Contracts with longer probation periods are unlikely, but if probation goes beyond 52 weeks there is a potential claim for unfair dismissal. However, an industrial tribunal has held that dismissal after 26 weeks (as the minimum period then was) but during probation could be fair if the employee is told of the probation period and the employer, though dissatisfied with the work, gives the employee a fair chance to improve (see *Hamblin* v. *London Borough of Ealing*, [1975] I.R.L.R. 354).

(iii) **Disciplinary practices and procedures**. If an employee is not engaged on an appropriate fixed term contract or on probation and has completed 52 weeks' service then the Code of Practice on Disciplinary Practices and Procedures issued by the Advisory Conciliation and Arbitration Service (ACAS) which came into effect on 20 June 1977 should be followed. ACAS is given power to issue codes of practice under the EPCA and they are available from regional directors of ACAS. Industrial tribunals take into account these codes of procedure, though they are not law, and it should be noted that the employer's case will be assisted if the practices and procedures have been agreed with a relevant trade union or staff association.

The main elements of the Code of Practice are as follows:

(a) *Joining instructions.* When a person joins the staff of an organisation he should be told what misdemeanors can lead to dismissal. These will vary from organisation to organisation but could include, for example, persistent lateness, careless work, and misuse of the telephone — we have all met employees who see no harm in using the firm's telephone to ring their relatives in New Zealand. New members of staff should also be told who has authority to give warnings under the Code of Practice and who may eventually dismiss them. In this connection it is preferable not to name too many persons who have this right and the right to dismiss should in particular be given to only one person, though this may be inconvenient in large firms.

(b) *Warnings*. The code envisages four stages under which the employee receives an oral warning, a written warning, and a final written warning to be followed by dismissal if there is no improvement by the employee.

In this connection it should be noted that a dismissal after the first warning will normally be regarded as unfair, though there may be circumstances in which an employee can be dismissed without a warning at all if there is gross misconduct. Thus in *Newman* v. *Alarmco*, [1976] I.R.L.R. 45 one of the company's employees had been living with his secretary and they demonstrated their affection for each other in the office, being seen frequently kissing and cuddling on the employer's premises during business hours, and on a particular occasion during business hours they were seen falling to the floor together after the secretary had tried to put jam on the employee's face. An Industrial Tribunal held that the employee's dismissal was fair since his association with his secretary was made evident during office hours and at the office itself. A warning was not required since the conduct concerned had been going on for some months and the employee must have known that it was likely to bring discredit upon the employer.

It is also advisable that any action taken by the employer after the first warning should be recorded in writing and where the facts of a case are doubtful it is better not to proceed to further warnings but rather to suspend the employee on full pay whilst proper investigations are carried out.

(c) *Appeals procedure.* The code also requires some form of appeals procedure to which the employee may have access after a warning which might lead to dismissal. Obviously an appeals procedure is not acceptable if the appeal is to a person or persons who can give warnings or eventually dismiss the employee and it might be thought right to allow the employee to go to a director, works manager, or at least senior shop steward level, in regard to an appeal.

There is, of course, a further reason for keeping all records relating to employee dismissal in writing, partly because the employee is entitled to a written statement setting out the reasons for his dismissal and also because industrial tribunals are more likely to be convinced by an employer's case if it is well set out in writing.

(iv) **Grievance procedures.** The Code of Practice also refers to individual grievance procedures. A simple grievance procedure which is rapid in its operation and settles a complaint fairly is well worth establishing because it can avoid the unpleasantness associated with disciplinary procedures and will in most cases obviate the need for dismissal. The Code suggests that the employee's grievance will be discussed at the first level with the employee's immediate superior, followed by a discussion at management level as a next stage at which the employee should be allowed a representative, e.g. a trade union official, followed by a right of appeal which may be to the same group of persons who deal with disciplinary matters.

DISCRIMINATORY DISMISSAL

In addition to legislation relating to unfair dismissal generally the Sex Discrimination Act, 1975 and the Race Relations Act, 1976 deal with complaints to industrial tribunals for dismissal on the grounds of sex, marital status, or race. In addition, dismissals of persons with spent convictions are dealt with by the Rehabilitation of Offenders Act, 1974.

The nature and scope of these provisions has already been considered and it is only necessary to add here that there are provisions in s 76 of the EPCA which prevent double compensation being paid, once under the SDA or the RRA and once under the general unfair dismissal provisions of the EPCA.

As we have seen, there are no statutory enforcement procedures for discrimination under the Rehabilitation of Offenders Act, 1974. Dismissal of persons with spent convictions can therefore only be relevant where a claim for summary dismissal is made at common law (see p. 109) or as part of a case presented to an industrial tribunal for unfair dismissal.

REDUNDANCY

The Redundancy Payments Act of 1965 (as amended by the EPCA) gives an employee a right to compensation by way of a redundancy payment if he is dismissed because of a redundancy.

1. **Meaning of redundancy.** Redundancy occurs where the services of employees are dispensed with because the employer ceases, or intends to cease, carrying on business, or does not require so many employees to do work of a certain kind. Employees who have been laid off or kept on short time without pay for four consecutive weeks (or for six weeks in a period of 13 weeks) are entitled to a redundancy payment if there is no reasonable prospect that normal working will be resumed.

Whilst dealing with the meaning of redundancy it should be noted that it may be possible to make two redundancies out of the abolition of one post.

ROBINSON v. BRITISH ISLAND AIRWAYS, *The Times*, 29 October 1977: Employment Appeal Tribunal

Facts

BIA carried out a genuine reorganisation of their workforce and as part of this eliminated the post of Flight Operations Manager held by Captain Robinson. His duties and those of another employee, the General Manager Operations and Traffic, were absorbed into a new post entitled Operations Manager. BIA alleged that Captain Robinson and the General Manager Operations and Traffic did not have the qualities suitable for the new post and both were made redundant. Captain Robinson then claimed that he had been unfairly dismissed on the ground that if only one post was abolished there could not be two redundancies arising from that abolition.

Judgment

The Employment Appeal Tribunal found that Captain Robinson was in fact redundant. His dismissal was attributable to the fact that the requirements of BIA's business for employees to carry out work of a particular kind had ceased or diminished and Captain Robinson and his fellow-employee were redundant.

2. **Eligibility**. Employees who have completed two years' continuous service are eligible for a redundancy payment. Additionally, they must work 16 hours or more per week (or eight hours or more where the employment has been for five years or more). Claims must be made within six months of the ending of the employment, though this time limit may be waived in appropriate circumstances by an industrial tribunal.

An employee who accepts an offer of suitable alternative employment with his employer is not entitled to a redundancy payment. Where a new offer is made, there is a trial period of four weeks following the making of the offer, during which the employer or the employee may end the contract while retaining all rights and liabilities under redundancy legislation. An employee who unreasonably refuses an offer of alternative employment is not entitled to a redundancy payment. Thus in *Fuller* v. *Stephanie Bowman*, [1977] I.R.L.R. 87, F was employed as a secretary at SB's premises which were situated in Mayfair. These premises attracted a very high rent and rates and so SB moved their offices to premises in Soho. These premises were situated over a sex shop and F refused the offer of renewed employment at the same salary and then brought a claim before an Industrial Tribunal for a redundancy payment. The Industrial Tribunal held that the question of unreasonableness was a matter of fact for the Tribunal and F's refusal to work over the sex shop was unreasonable so that she was not entitled to a redundancy payment.

3. **Amount of redundancy payment.** Those aged 41 to 65 (60 women) receive one and a half week's pay (up to a maximum of £100 per week) for each year of service up to a maximum of 20 years. In other age groups the above provisions apply except that the week's pay changes, i.e. for those

aged 22 to 40 it is one week's pay and for those 15 to 21 it is a half week's pay.

Employees over 64 (59 women) have their redundancy payment reduced progressively so that for each complete month by which the age exceeds 64 (or 59) on the Saturday of the week on which the contract ends, the normal entitlement is reduced by one-twelfth. Complaints by employees in respect of the right to a redundancy payment, or questions as to its amount, may, as we have seen, be made to an industrial tribunal which will make a declaration as to the employee's rights which form the basis on which payment can be recovered from the employer.

4. **Rebates for employers.** Employers who have made a redundancy payment may claim a rebate from the Redundancy Fund, the details of which are set out in Sched. 6 of the EPCA.

To obtain the rebate the employer must notify the local office of the Department of Employment that he intends to make a claim, three weeks or more before the expected date of dismissal if ten or more employees are involved, or two weeks or more in the case of redundancies involving less than ten employees. If the employer fails to give adequate prior notice of his intention to claim a rebate the Secretary of State may reduce that rebate.

5. **Procedure for handling redundancies.** This is as follows:
(a) *Notification.* Employers must notify the Department of Employment of redundancies being planned which would involve the dismissal of more than ten employees in a period of one month. The minimum notification period is 30 days. This notification period is different from the one referred to in 4 above. If the employer fails to notify the Secretary of State of proposed redundancies, the Secretary of State may reduce the redundancy payments rebate or a magistrates court may impose a fine on the employer.
(b) *Consultation.* Employers are required to consult with trade union representatives as soon as possible which (in line with EEC requirements), if 100 or more employees are affected, is not less than 30 days before the redundancies take effect, or 30 days if ten or more employees are affected. Consultation involves the employer in telling the unions the reasons for the proposals, together with the number and type of employees to be dismissed, the total number of employees of that type at the establishment involved, the proposed method of selection and of carrying out the dismissals.

Representations made by the unions must be received and replied to. If this is not done, an industrial tribunal may, on the complaint of a trade union (or in a multi-union situation, by any one of them), make a declaration of the tribunal's findings, and the tribunal may make a 'protective award' under which the employees will be kept in employment and paid for not more than a period corresponding to the minimum time required for prior consultation, that is, as we have already seen, 30 days. If an employee is not paid during all or part of the period for which the protective award applies, he or his union may apply to an industrial tribunal, which will issue an order to the employer to pay the amount of remuneration due to the employee.

An employer is excused from consultation with a trade union in what s 99 of the Employment Protection Act, 1975 (which is still in force) refers to as 'special circumstances'. It appears that the insolvency of the employer is not a special circumstance for this purpose.

Thus in *Baker's Union* v. *Clarks of Hove Ltd.* [1978] I.R.L.R. 366 the Court of Appeal decided that an employer who makes employees redundant because he is ceasing to trade on the ground of insolvency, followed by the appointment of a receiver, is not excused from consulting with the trade union representatives of his employees. The matter reached the Court of Appeal from the Employment Appeal Tribunal which had decided that insolvency was a special circumstance excusing consultation. The Industrial Tribunal had found that it was not and was prepared to make a protective award for some 368 employees of Clarks under which in addition to redundancy pay the employer was required to pay the employees concerned remuneration for a protected period. The claim was important because remuneration payable under a protective award is a preferential debt in an insolvency such as a liquidation or receivership.

Clarks agreed that they had failed to consult the union about redundancy as required by the Act but they said that they should be excused because there were special circumstances, i.e. a situation of insolvency which made it not reasonably practicable to comply and that there was nothing they could have done to comply. The special circumstances, Clarks said, were the grave financial difficulties which the company was in during the autumn of 1976. The directors had tried to raise money but could not do so and on 24 October 1976 they stopped trading. Had they not done so they might have been personally liable for the company's debts during any further period of trading under s 332 of the Companies Act, 1948. A receiver was appointed on 27 October 1976.

The Court of Appeal could not accept that on the facts of the case the insolvency was a special circumstance because it was merely the culmination of a gradual run-down of the company and was not a sudden disaster. To be 'special' a circumstance had to be uncommon and the Industrial Tribunal had come to the right decision, i.e. that Clarks had not sustained the defence of special circumstances so that the protective award was payable.

(c) *Collective agreements on redundancy*. The Secretary of State may, on the application of the employer and the unions involved, make an order modifying the requirements of redundancy pay legislation if he is satisfied that there is a collective agreement which makes satisfactory alternative arrangements for dealing with redundancies. The provisions of the agreement must be 'on the whole at least as favourable' as the statutory provisions, and must include, in particular, arrangements allowing an employee to go to independent arbitration or to make a complaint to an industrial tribunal.

6. **Persons excluded from the Act.** Some employees are specifically excluded from the provisions of redundancy legislation. In particular, an employee who works under a contract of employment for a fixed term of two years or more may agree to exclude the right to claim for a redundancy payment if the term is not renewed when the original contract expires. Other persons excluded from the provisions of redundancy legislation are registered dockworkers, public officers and civil servants, and situations in which a husband employs his wife or *vice versa.*

In addition it should be noted that in *North East Coast Ship Repairers* v. *Secretary of State for Employment*, [1978] I.C.R. 755 the Employment Appeal Tribunal held that an apprentice who, having completed the period of his apprenticeship finds that the firm cannot provide him with work, is not entitled to a redundancy payment. This case has relevance for trainees and others completing contracts in order to obtain relevant practical experience.

OTHER METHODS OF TERMINATION OF A CONTRACT OF SERVICE

Having considered the termination of the contract by unfair or discriminatory dismissal or redundancy we must now turn to other ways in which the contract of service may be brought to an end. These are set out below.

By Notice

A contract of service can be brought to an end by either party giving notice to the other, although where the employer gives notice even in accordance with the contract of service or under the statutory provisions of the EPCA he may still face a claim for unfair dismissal or a redundancy payment.

The most important practical aspect is the length of notice to be given by the parties, in particular the employer. The EPCA contains statutory provisions in regard to *minimum* periods of notice and the only relevance of the express provisions of a particular contract of service on the matter are that a contract may provide for longer periods of notice than does the Act. Under s 49 of the EPCA an employee is entitled to one week's notice after four weeks' service; after two years' service the minimum entitlement is increased to two weeks, and for each year of service after that it is increased by one week up to a maximum of 12 weeks' notice after 12 years' service. An employee who is engaged for a specific job on a 12-week or shorter contract is not entitled to any notice unless in the event the contract is extended or he is retained for a period longer than 12 weeks.

An employee, once he has been employed for four weeks, must give his employer one week's notice and the period of one week's notice applies for the duration of the contract so far as the employee is concerned, no matter how long he has served the employer.

The period of employment must be continuous and Sched. 13 of the EPCA defines continuous employment for this purpose to include periods when an employee is in fact absent from work, e.g. when sick or injured, or because of pregnancy. It is, perhaps, of special interest to note that periods of absence because of a strike or lock-out by the employer count as continuous employment for the purposes of notice.

Breach of the provisions relating to minimum periods of notice do not involve an employer in any penalty, but the rights conferred by the Act will be taken into account in assessing the employer's liability for breach of contract. Thus an employer who has dismissed his employee without due notice is generally liable for the wages due to the employee for the appropriate period of notice at the contract rate.

It should be noted that the EPCA provisions regarding notice do not affect the common law rights of an employer to dismiss an employee summarily without notice for misconduct, e.g. disobedience, neglect or drunkenness (see p. 99).

In practice, a contract of service is often terminated by a payment in lieu of notice and this is permitted by s 49 of the EPCA.

By Agreement

As in any other contract, the parties to a contract of employment may terminate the contract by agreement. Thus if employer and employee agree to new terms and conditions on, e.g. a promotion of the employee, the old agreement is discharged and superseded by the new one.

An employee could agree to be 'bought off' by his employer under an agreement to discharge the existing contract of service. In this connection it should be noted that discharge of a contract of service by agreement is not a 'dismissal' for the purposes, e.g. of an unfair dismissal claim, but should a claim for unfair dismissal be brought by an employee who has been 'bought off' the industrial tribunal concerned will want to see evidence of a genuine and fair agreement by employer and employee and may allow a claim of unfair dismissal if the discharging agreement is one-sided and biased in favour of the employer.

By Passage of Time

In the case of a fixed-term contract, e.g. where an employee is engaged for, say, three years, the contract will terminate at the end of the three years though there may be provisions for notice within that period.

By Frustration

We have already considered frustration of the contract of service by incapacity such as illness (see p. 93). However, other events can bring about the discharge of the contract of service by frustration.

HARE v. MURPHY BROTHERS, [1975] 3 All E.R. 940: Court of Appeal

Facts

Hare, a foreman, after 25 years' service in Murphy's employment was sentenced to 12 months' imprisonment for unlawful wounding during an incident wholly unconnected with his work. Evidence was given at his trial that if Hare was not sent to prison he would get his job back; otherwise the question would have to be considered on his release. On his release he was told that his post had been filled and the company had no other vacancy for him. They did, however, make him an *ex gratia* payment of £150. Hare then claimed a redundancy payment and the matter eventually went to the Court of Appeal.

Judgment

It was held by the Court of Appeal, dismissing the application, that the sentence was of such length and Hare's position of such importance that the sentence rendered it impossible for Hare to perform his part of the contract of employment and the contract was accordingly terminated by frustration as from the date of the sentence so that there was no entitlement to a redundancy payment.

Furthermore, *death* of either employer or employee will discharge the contract by frustration from the date of the death so that, for example, the personal representatives of the employer are not required to continue the contract. However, the employee's estate has a claim for wages or salary due to the date of death.

Under the EPCA claims for unfair dismissal arising before the employer's death survive and may be brought after the death of the employer against his estate. Furthermore, the death of an employer is usually regarded as a 'dismissal' for redundancy purposes and the employee may make a claim against the employer's estate.

Partnership Dissolution

A person who is employed by a partnership which is dissolved is regarded as dismissed on dissolution of the firm. There is no claim for unfair dismissal or redundancy pay but the dismissal is regarded as wrongful at common law and there may be a claim by the employee for damages, but these will be nominal only if the partnership business continues and the continuing partners offer new employment on the old terms.

BRACE v. CALDER, [1895] 2 Q.B. 253: Queen's Bench Division

Facts

The defendants, a partnership consisting of four members, agreed to employ the plaintiff as manager of a branch of the business for two years. Five months later the partnership was dissolved by the retirement of two of the partners and the business was transferred to the other two who offered to employ the plaintiff on the same terms as before, but he refused the offer. The plaintiff brought an action for breach of contract seeking to recover the salary he would have received had he served the whole period of two years.

Judgment

It was held that the dissolution of the partnership constituted a wrongful dismissal of the plaintiff but that he was entitled only to nominal damages since it was unreasonable to have rejected the offer of continued employment.

A partnership is dissolved whenever one partner dies or becomes bankrupt or leaves the firm for any reason. However, the EPCA provides for continuity of employment of employees who continue to work for the new firm.

Appointment of a Receiver

Where a company has borrowed money and given security for the loan by charging its assets under a debenture, the debenture holders may if, e.g. they are not paid interest on the loan, appoint a receiver and manager. The most common appointment is by a bank in respect of a loan to a company.

If the receiver is appointed under the terms of the debenture he is normally made agent of the company and, where this is so, employees of the company are not dismissed on his appointment (*re Mack Trucks Ltd*, [1967] 1 W.L.R. 780) and their employment is continuous for the purposes of employment legislation. Employees are, however, dismissed if the receiver sells the undertaking (*re Foster Clarke Ltd's Indenture Trusts*, [1966] 1 W.L.R. 125) or where continuance of the employee's contract would be inconsistent with the appointment of a receiver, as could be the case in regard to the contract of a managing director. However, even a managing director may not be regarded as dismissed where the receiver has a part-time appointment (*Griffiths* v. *Secretary of State for Social Services*, [1973] 3 All E.R. 1184).

If the appointment is made by the court then the receiver is not the agent of the company but an officer of the court, and his appointment operates to terminate the contracts of all employees and the continuity of their employment ceases and they have a claim for damages for breach of contract. The receiver may, of course, continue the employment by offering what are in effect new contracts but where this is so there is a break in the continuity of employment for the purposes of employment legislation.

Company Liquidation

There are three possibilities as follows:

(a) **A compulsory winding up.** Here the court orders the winding up of the company, usually on the petition of a creditor because it cannot pay his debt. The making of a compulsory winding up order by the court may have the following effects according to the circumstances of the case:

(i) Where the company's business ceases the winding up order will operate as a wrongful dismissal of employees.

(ii) Where the liquidator continues the business he may be regarded as an agent of the company so that the employment continues or, alternatively, the court may regard the appointment of the liquidator as a giving of notice to the employee who then works out that notice under the liquidator. It is, however, the better view that employees may, if they so choose, regard themselves as unfairly dismissed because the company has ceased to employ them, the new contract being with the liquidator.

(b) **A voluntary winding up.** This commences on the resolution of the members and if the company's business ceases there is a wrongful dismissal of employees. If the company's business continues the position would appear to be as set out in (a)(ii) above.

(c) **A voluntary winding up to reconstruct or amalgamate with another company**. This, it appears, does not operate as a dismissal of employees (*Midland Counties District Bank* v. *Attwood*, [1905] Ch. 357).

Bankruptcy

The bankruptcy of the employer or, indeed, of the employee, does not automatically discharge the contract of service, though it will if there is a term to that effect in the agreement. Thus the employment can continue, though in practical terms it may be impossible to pay employees wages, and in this case they will be discharged and be able to claim damages for wrongful dismissal, and also in the bankruptcy for wages accrued due in regard to which they have a preferential claim in the bankruptcy.

A trustee in bankruptcy cannot insist that an employee continue in service because the contract is one of a personal nature. The bankruptcy of an employee will not normally affect the contract of service unless there is a term to that effect in the contract. Company directors provide a special case since the articles of most companies provide for termination of the office on becoming bankrupt.

WRONGFUL AND SUMMARY DISMISSAL AT COMMON LAW

The claim at common law for wrongful dismissal is based upon a general principle of the law of contract, i.e. wrongful repudiation of the contract of service by the employer.

The common law action has, of course, been largely superseded by the statutory provisions relating to unfair dismissal and a common law claim is only likely to be brought by an employee who has a fixed term contract at a high salary. Thus a company director who has a fixed term contract for, say, three years at a salary of, say, £25,000 per annum, might, if wrongfully dismissed, find it more profitable in terms of damages obtainable to sue at common law for breach of contract, though the employer may be able to resist the claim where the employee was guilty, e.g. of misconduct, disobedience, or immorality.

In other cases where the contract of service is not for a fixed term there is no claim for damages at common law provided the employer gives proper notice or pays wages in lieu, though in such a case the employee has at least potentially a claim for unfair dismissal which he could pursue. Again, the employer may resist a claim for unfair dismissal on the basis of misconduct, disobedience, or immorality, and we have already given some consideration to these matters in the context of statutory unfair dismissal. Since the issue of a justifiable dismissal is now normally raised in the context of a statutory claim for unfair dismissal, it is not proposed to deal further with cases justifying a dismissal at common law which might be raised as a defence to a claim at common law for wrongful dismissal.

RIGHTS AND REMEDIES ON DISMISSAL

These are as follows:

Written Statement of Reasons for Dismissal

At common law an employer is not required to give his employee any reasons for dismissal. However, s 53 of the EPCA provides that where an employee is dismissed, with or without notice, or by failure to renew a contract for a fixed term, he shall be provided by his employer on request within 14 days of that request with a written statement giving particulars of the reasons for his dismissal. This provision applies only to employees who have been continuously employed for a period of 26 weeks. The written statement is admissible in evidence in any proceedings relating to the dismissal and if an employer refuses to give a written statement the employee may complain to an industrial tribunal. If the tribunal upholds the complaint it may make a declaration as to what it finds the employer's reasons were for dismissing the employee and must make an award of two weeks' pay to the employee.

Employer's Insolvency

If the employer is bankrupt or dies insolvent or where the employer is a company and is in liquidation, the unpaid wages or salary of a clerk or servant have priority as to payment, as have the wages of a labourer or workman, but in each case only to a maximum of £800 and limited to services rendered during the period of four months before the commencement of the insolvency. Any balance over £800 or four months ranks as an ordinary debt. Also preferential is accrued holiday remuneration payable to a clerk, servant or workman or labourer on the termination of his employment before or because of the insolvency.

The EPCA adds to the above preferential debts by including in the list sums owed in respect of statutory guarantee payments, guaranteed payments during statutory time off, remuneration on suspension for medical grounds, or remuneration under a protective award given because of failure to consult properly on a redundancy.

It should also be noted that under s 122 of the EPCA an employee may in the case of his employer's insolvency make a claim on the Redundancy Fund rather than relying on the preferential payments procedure set out above. If the employee is paid from the Redundancy Fund the Secretary of State for Employment may then claim as a preferential creditor in the employer's insolvency for the amount paid out of the Redundancy Fund.

The limits of the employee's claim are as follows:

(a) Arrears of pay for a period not exceeding eight weeks with a maximum of £100 per week.

(b) Holiday pay with a limit of six weeks and £100 per week.

(c) Payments in lieu of notice at a rate not exceeding £100 per week.

(d) Payment outstanding for unfair dismissal.

It should also be noted that claims on the Redundancy Fund will not normally be admitted if the liquidator or trustee in bankruptcy can satisfy the Secretary of State that the preferential payments will be paid from funds available in the insolvency and without undue delay.

Damages for Wrongful Dismissal

These are covered by common law rules and will be looked at in the context of the fixed term contract which has been wrongfully repudiated by the employer before the term has expired. The damages will be the amount of money which the employee would have earned under the contract, less the amount of money which he could reasonably have expected to earn elsewhere. Arrears of pay for work done prior to dismissal, if any, are also included.

The general principle of the common law that a plaintiff suing for breach of contract must mitigate his loss applies and reference should be made at this point to the case of *Brace* v. *Calder*, (1895) (see p. 107).

Damages for loss of benefits other than salary may be included, e.g. a rent-free house, provided these were mandatory rights in the contract of service. There is no claim for discretionary benefits which an employer may or may not give, such as discretionary bonuses.

It should also be noted that since damages for wrongful dismissal normally involve an assessment of lost salary, a deduction for income tax must be made before the plaintiff receives his award (see Income and Corporation Taxes Act, 1970, ss 187-188 and s 24, Finance Act, 1978).

Furthermore, sums which the employer would have had to deduct from salary for Social Security contributions and any unemployment benefit received by the employee will also go to reduce damages but National Assistance payments received by the employee are not deducted from the damages since they are discretionary. In addition, sums which the employee has received by way of redundancy payments also go to reduce the damages

(*Stocks* v. *Magna Merchants Ltd*, [1973] I.C.R. 530) and so it would seem on the basis of *Stocks* do amounts received by the employee in respect of a claim for unfair dismissal.

The Equitable Remedies of Specific Performance and Injunction

A decree of specific performance is an order of the court and constitutes an express instruction to a party to a contract to perform the actual obligation which he undertook under its terms. If the person who is subject to the order fails to comply with it, he is in contempt of court and potentially liable to be fined or imprisoned until he complies with the order and thus purges his contempt. For all practical purposes the remedy is not given to enforce performance of a contract of service.

An injunction is an order of the court whereby an individual is required to refrain from the further doing of the act complained of. Again, a person who is subject to such an order and fails to comply with it is in contempt of court and the consequences listed above follow from the contempt. An injunction may be used to prevent many wrongful acts, e.g. the torts of trespass and nuisance, but in the context of contract the remedy will be granted to enforce a negative stipulation in a contract in a situation where it would be unjust to confine the plaintiff to damages. In a proper case an injunction may be used as an indirect method of enforcing a contract for personal services, such as a contract of employment, but in that case a clear negative stipulation is required.

The following cases provide illustrations of the application of the negative stipulation rule.

WHITWOOD CHEMICAL CO. v. HARDMAN, [1891] 2 Ch. 416: Court of Appeal

Facts

The defendant entered into a contract of service with the plaintiffs and agreed to give the whole of his time to them. In fact he occasionally worked for others, and the plaintiffs tried to enforce the undertaking in the contract of service by an injunction.

Judgment

It was held by the Court of Appeal that an injunction could not be granted because there was no express negative stipulation. The defendant had merely stated what he would do, and not what he would not do, and to read into the undertaking an agreement not to work for anyone else required the Court to imply a negative stipulation from a positive one. No such implication could be made.

WARNER BROTHERS PICTURES INCORPORATED v. NELSON, [1937] 1 K.B. 209: King's Bench Division

Facts

The defendant, the film actress Bette Davis, had entered into a contract in which she agreed to act exclusively for the plaintiffs for 12 months. She was anxious to obtain more money and so she left America and entered into a contract with a person in England. The plaintiffs now asked for an injunction restraining the defendant from carrying out the English contract.

Judgment

It was held by Branson, J. that an injunction would be granted. The contract in fact contained a negative stipulation not to work for anyone else and this could be enforced. However, since the contract was an American one, the Court limited the operation of the injunction to the area of the Court's jurisdiction, and although the contract stipulated that the defendant would not work in any other occupation, the injunction was confined to work on stage or screen.

In this connection it should also be noted that s 16 of the Trade Union and Labour Relations Act, 1974 provides that no court shall by way of specific performance or an injunction compel an employee to do any work or attend any place for the doing of any work. Thus the Act is in line with the judicial approach to specific performance but to some extent out of line with the judicial approach to the granting of an injunction. Thus the availability of an injunction in cases involving contracts of service is subject to the provisions of s 16 of the 1974 Act, and although the matter has not been worked out by the courts it would seem that on general principles the granting of an injunction in the context of a contract of employment is no longer possible since statute law is superior in terms of its applicability to decisions of the judiciary.

Employee's Breach of Contract

An employer may sue his employees for damages for breach of the contract of service by the employee. Such claims are potentially available for, e.g. damage to the employer's proprty, as where machinery is damaged by negligent operation (*Baster* v. *London & County Printing Works*, [1899] 1 Q.B.

901), or for refusal to work resulting in damage by lost production (*National Coal Board* v. *Galley*, [1958] 1 W.L.R. 16). Such claims are rare and impractical because of the fact that the employee will not in most cases be able to meet the claim and also, and perhaps more importantly, because they lead to industrial unrest. In these circumstances we shall not pursue the matter further.

Dual Jurisdiction of Industrial Tribunals

It should be noted that under the EPCA, s 131, an industrial tribunal is given power to incorporate the rules of the common law in its judgments relating to contracts of service. Thus while it is considering a claim for unfair dismissal it may also take into account the rights of the parties at common law in terms of a wrongful dismissal. It cannot award specific performance or an injunction, nor can it deal with damages for personal injuries. However, the section is useful because it prevents what could be an inconvenient division of the common law and statutory rulings in regard to contracts of employment.

EEC REQUIREMENTS — A BRIEF COMPARISON

There are three main areas of the UK employment provisions which can be directly compared with the position in the EEC. In the order in which we have dealt with these matters in this text they are as follows:

(a) **Pregnant employees.** Pregnant employees are protected against dismissal in some countries in the EEC, e.g. West Germany, France, Italy, Belgium, and Luxembourg, and there are also provisions giving maternity leave entitlement. In general terms, statutory payments during maternity leave are paid by the state and the UK level of payments is amongst the most generous.

As regards reinstatement after pregnancy, this exists in West Germany, France, and Italy, and in each case the employee may claim reinstatement for up to one year after confinement.

(b) **Paternity leave.** This does not exist in the UK but there are provisions allowing it in France and Belgium, the period of leave which can be claimed being three days and two days respectively.

(c) **Unfair dismissal.** There are provisions relating to unfair dismissal in other countries of the EEC, though the UK's approach, which is to consider reinstatement or re-engagement as a first option, is not universally followed elsewhere. Money compensation is the more usual remedy, and only in West

Germany and Italy is reinstatement or re-engagement considered as a first remedy.

(d) **Redundancy**. There is an EEC Directive on redundancies which requires consultation and notification. The EPCA improves upon the Directive by requiring a longer period of notification/consultation than the Directive, i.e. 60 instead of 30 days. (This is now amended to 30 days.)

Procedure differs so that, for example, in Belgium a works council decides the basis of redundancy in terms of selection of employees to be made redundant, and in West Germany a works council and the employer must reach agreement on the way in which a particular redundancy situation is to be handled. In France employers are required by law to have a redundancy procedure agreement but this is subject to state intervention in a particular redundancy situation, and any alternative solution proposed by the state must be accepted and takes precedence over the redundancy procedure agreement.

4 Collective Agreements and Statutory Awards

COLLECTIVE AGREEMENTS — GENERALLY

Having considered the general principles of the contract of employment it is necessary to give a brief treatment of collective agreements, since the terms and conditions of service of many employees are affected by what are known as collective agreements made between one or more trade unions and one or more employers' associations, as a result of what is termed collective bargaining.

In terms of enforceability before a court of law, the legal status of these arguments is dealt with by s. 18 of the Trade Union and Labour Relations Act, 1974, which provides that a collective agreement will be presumed *not* to create legal relations unless it is in writing and contains a provision saying that the agreement is enforceable in whole or in regard to named parts of it. It will be found that most collective agreements are binding in honour only and, if not honoured by employer or trade union, cannot be the subject of an action at law.

STATUTORY PROVISIONS ENCOURAGING COLLECTIVE BARGAINING

Certain statutory provisions exist to encourage collective bargaining. These are set out below.

Recognition of Trade Unions (Employment Protection Act, 1975, SS. 11-16)

Trade unions which are independent of the employer may, if the employer will not negotiate with them, refer the issue of recognition to the Advisory Conciliation and Arbitration Service (ACAS), which will attempt to resolve the matter by conciliation. If this fails, ACAS may recommend that the employer should recognise the union concerned. If the employer fails to do so ACAS may refer the matter to the Central Arbitration Committee (CAC), and the CAC may make an award setting out what the terms and conditions of employment of the employees concerned are, and the employer is required to observe these, even though they may have been imposed upon him unilaterally.

Disclosure of Information (EPA, 1975, SS. 17-21)

An employer is required to disclose information which is necessary for the purposes of collective bargaining and for the purposes of good industrial relations to representatives of recognised and independent trade unions. If the employer fails to disclose, the trade union concerned may complain to the CAC which may, in the last analysis, make an award of the terms and conditions of service which then form part of the contract of employment of the employees concerned and which the employer is required to observe.

ACAS Code of Practice 2, which was brough into force on 22 August 1977 (see SI 1977/937), gives examples of information which it would be relevant to disclose as follows:

(a) **Pay and benefits**, e.g. the principles and structure of the payment system.

(b) **Conditions of service**, e.g. training and promotion.

(c) **Manpower**, e.g. numbers employed analysed according to grade.

(d) **Performance**, e.g. productivity and efficiency data.

(e) **Financial information**, i.e. cost structure, gross and net profits, sources of earnings, assets, liabilities, allocation of profits, details of Government financial assistance, transfer prices, loans to parent or subsidiary companies, and interest charged.

The Setting up of ACAS and the CAC (EPA, 1975, SS. 1-6 and Sched. 1 and S. 10 and Sched. 1)

ACAS is an independent statutory body controlled by a council, the members of which are appointed by the Secretary of State for Employment after consultation with both sides of industry, i.e. employers and unions. The functions of ACAS include the extension of collective bargaining and the improvement of industrial relations. In addition, its conciliation officers have the function of seeking to settle complaints referred to industrial tribunals before they are heard by the tribunal concerned.

CAC is composed of members representing employers and workers and acts as an arbitrator on trade disputes referred to it by ACAS. Its major functions are concerned with trade union recognition and the disclosure of information by employers.

Collective Agreements and Contracts of Service

The terms of a collective agreement may be incorporated into individual contracts of service *expressly*. Where this is so, the terms and conditions are according to the latest collective agreement and thus will be varied from time to time.

The terms of a collective agreement may also be *implied*, as where it has been acted upon without express incorporation. However, in view of the present provisions of the law requiring written particulars of the contract of employment which may refer to a collective agreement, express incorporation is, these days, more likely, and no further consideration will be given to the case law on implied incorporation.

As regards 'no strike' clauses in collective agreements, s. 18(4) of the Trade Union and Labour Relations Act, 1974 applies and provides that clauses in collective agreements which restrict strikes or other industrial action by workers will not be incorporated into individual contracts of service unless the collective agreement

(a) is in writing; and

(b) states expressly that the 'no strike' clauses are liable to be incorporated; and
(c) is reasonably available to the workers affected at their place of work and is available to be consulted during their working hours.

STATUTORY AWARDS

The reason for a brief examination of these is that, like a collective agreement, a statutory award relating to terms and conditions of employment becomes incorporated into individual contracts of employment. The awards are considered under the headings set out below.

Extension of Terms and Conditions

Under s. 97, EPCA, 1978 a trade union or an employers' association may make a claim to ACAS under Para. 1 of Sched. 11 to the EPA, 1975 that an employer is failing to comply with recognised minimum terms and conditions which have been negotiated for workers in comparable jobs in a particular trade or industry. Thus failure by an employer to abide by a collective agreement can be the subject of a claim.

In addition, if there are no such recognised minimum terms and conditions, a claim may be made as above which refers simply to the general level of terms and conditions of workers in comparable jobs. Thus, even where there is no collective agreement, a claim may be made on the above basis.

If ACAS cannot settle the claim on a voluntary basis it is referred to the CAC which, if it regards the claim as good, will make an award of terms and conditions of employment which then form part of the contract of employment of the workers involved.

In a Wages Council industry (see below) or in agriculture, an independent trade union may make a claim to ACAS where a member of that union is receiving less than the minimum rate being paid to workers doing comparable jobs in the same industry, so long as the union concerned has negotiated a collective agreement which covers a significant number of employees in that industry.

Wages Councils, Statutory Joint Industrial Councils and Agriculture

The system of Wages Councils, which has its roots in legislation passed at the beginning of the twentieth century, has the object of incorporating terms and conditions of service into individual contracts of employment where voluntary bargaining does not properly secure suitable terms and conditions for the workers in a particular type of employment, such as catering.

The Wages Councils Act, 1979 consolidates previous law and allows the Secretary of State or a Commision of Inquiry to establish wages councils for industries where there is no proper machinery for regulating terms and conditions of employment.

Under the Act of 1979 ACAS takes over the functions of the old Commission of Inquiry and the powers of Wages Councils are increased so that they can fix terms and conditions of employment generally and are not confined, as before, to pay and holidays. The powers of the Agricultural Wages Board are similarly increased.

The Secretary of State can convert a Wages Council into what is called a Statutory Joint Industrial Council by excluding the independent members of the wages council concerned, leaving only representatives of workers and employers. He may, in addition, abolish a statutory joint industrial council if he feels that there is adequate collective bargaining within the industry.

Ss. 10-12 of the 1979 Act give the Secretary of State power to encourage the development of collective bargaining in wages councils industries.

The Fair Wages Resolution

The Fair Wages Resolution was passed by the House of Commons in 1946 and it instructs Government departments to insist on fair wages clauses in contracts made by them with contractors who should agree to abide by collective agreements, and to guarantee observance of these also by any sub-contractor. Enforcement is a matter for the Government department concerned, which can iinsist on arbitration if it feels a contractor is not observing the Resolution. This will, in most cases, lead to a change in the terms and conditions of the contractor's employees, but there is no general statutory provision which provides that this shall happen automatically.

5 Health, Safety and Welfare at Work

This chapter will concern itself with those provisions of the law which are designed to secure the health, safety and welfare of persons at work and the legal controls over industry in regard to the use of dangerous substances and emissions of noxious and/or offensive substances into the atmosphere.

HEALTH AND SAFETY AT WORK ACT, 1974

Employers' Duties to Employees (S. 2)

Generally

S. 2(1) of the Act states that it shall be the duty of every employer to ensure, so far as is reasonably practicable, the health, safety and welfare at work of his employees.

As regards health and safety of employees, there is, of course, a duty on the employer at common law in respect of these and an employee may be awarded damages in a *civil* action against his employer in respect of any injuries suffered because of his employer's default.

However, the sanctions of the 1974 Act are *criminal* in nature, and failure by an employer to comply with health, safety and welfare provisions can result in a sentence of up to two years' imprisonment and/or an unlimited fine. In addition, it should be noted that the Act applies to all places of work and not just to factories.

Particular duties

S. 2(2) states that the matters to which the employer's duty extends in *particular* but without prejudice to his fulfilling of the requirements of the general duty are as set out below.

(i) An employer must ensure the provision and maintenance of plant and systems of work that are, so far as is reasonably practicable, safe and without risks to health.

There is, of course, a similar duty at common law but, as we have seen, sanctions under the 1974 Act are criminal, so that an employer could be prosecuted for failing to maintain, e.g., an electric drill which flew apart and injured an employee, though it should be noted that the Act can be enforced even though no accident has occurred.

(ii) An employer must make arrangements for ensuring, so far as is reasonably practicable, safety and absence of risks to health in connection with the use, handling, storage and transport of articles and substances.

S. 53 states that 'article for use at work' means any plant designed for use or operation by persons at work and also any article designed for use as a component in any such plant. 'Substance' is defined as any natural or artificial substance, whether in solid or liquid form, or in the form of a gas or vapour.

(iii) An employer must provide such information, instruction, training and supervision as is necessary to ensure, so far as is reasonably practicable, the health and safety at work of his employees.

(iv) An employer must, so far as is reasonably practicable, as regards any place of work under his control, maintain it in a good condition that is safe and without risks to health and must provide and maintain means of access to and egress from the place of work which are safe and without risks.

As regards place of work, this would seem to be included with 'premises', and premises are defined as in s. 53 as including vehicles, vessels, aircraft or hovercraft as well as installations on land, any off-shore installation, and any other installation, whether floating or resting on the sea bed or the sub-soil thereof, or resting on other land covered with water or the sub-soil thereof. Any tent or moveable structure is also covered.

(v) An employer must provide and maintain a working environment for his employees that is, so far as is reasonably practicable, safe, without risks to health, and adequate as regards facilities and arrangements for the welfare of employees at work. As regards arrangements for welfare at work, this refers to the provision of amenities such as proper toilet facilities, canteens, heating, lighting, and ventilation.

It should be noted how wide-ranging are the duties set out in (i) to (v) above. They apply in factories, on oil rigs and even to the employer of a bread-roundsman who is, e.g., required to work in a van with a leaky exhaust which is a risk to the roundsman's health.

Statements of Policy (S. 2 and S. 79)

S. 2(3) provides that it shall be the duty of every employer to prepare and, as often as may be appropriate, revise a written statement of his general policy with respect to the health and safety at work of his employees and the organisation and arrangements for the time being in force for carrying out that policy, and to bring the statement and any revision of it to the notice of all his employees. Employers with fewer than five employees are exempt from the above requirements (S.I. 1975/1584). Others are liable to prosecution if there is no statement or if it is defective. An employer who fails to comply with the arrangements in his statement may also be prosecuted.

As regards *policy*, this seems to involve only a statement that it is the policy of the organisation to concern itself at all times with the health and safety of its employees. There must, of course, be an *organisation* to deal with health and safety and this involves the appointment, e.g., of safety committees, safety representatives, and possibly a safety officer.

The statement should deal with possible and inevitable hazards and dangerous occurrences at the workplace, and should explain to the employees how they can avoid accidents arising from them. The statement may be displayed on notice boards, but on the whole it is advisable to give a copy of the statement to each employee. Under s. 79 of the Act the Secretary of State may make regulations requiring directors' reports to contain information regarding arrangements in force during the year relating to health, safety and welfare of employees.

Duties of Employers and the Self-employed to Persons who are not their Employees (S. 3)

S. 3(1) provides that it shall be the duty of every employer to conduct his undertaking in such a way as to ensure, so far as is reasonably practicable, that persons not in his employment who may be affected thereby are not thereby exposed to risks to their health or safety. There is a similarly worded duty placed upon the self-employed by s. 3(2).

The section covers a wide variety of people, including customers in a shop, occupiers of a neighbouring premises, and even members of the public who pass the workplace.

Basically the section makes it a criminal offence — for which there may be a prosecution even though there is no injury to anyone — to run an organisation or undertaking *negligently* or so as to cause a *nuisance*. Thus if, e.g., a customer in a shop trips over a trailing wire left by a maintenance man there is a potential action in negligence for damages by the customer and the possibility of a prosecution under s. 3. Similarly, excessive noise or vibration from premises on which the undertaking is conducted may result in an action by an occupier of adjoining premises for nuisance and in a prosecution under s. 3.

Statements (S. 3)

S. 3(3) provides that in such cases as may be prescribed (and at the time of writing the Secretary of State has not prescribed) it shall be the duty of every employer and every self-employed person, in the prescribed circumstances, and in the prescribed manner, to give to persons who are not his employees, who may be affected by the way in which he conducts his undertaking, the prescribed information about such aspects of the way in which he conducts his undertaking as might affect their health or safety.

When the Secretary of State prescribes, therefore, those employers and those self-employed persons concerned will have to tell, e.g., those coming on to their premises how to avoid accidents.

Premises — Duties of Employers and the Self-employed to Non-Employees (S. 4)

S. 4(1) states that certain duties are imposed upon persons in relation to other persons who are not their employees who use non-domestic premises made available to them as a place of work or as a place where they may use plant or substances provided for their use there. The duties are set out in s. 4(2) which states that it shall be the duty of each person who has to any extent control of premises as referred to above or of the means of access to them or egress from them, or of any plant or substance in such premises to take such measures as it is reasonably practical for a person in his position to take to ensure, so far as is reasonably practicable, that the premises, or means of access thereto or egress therefrom available for use by persons using the premises and any plant or substance in the premises or, as the case may be, provided for use there, is or are safe and without risks to health. S. 4(3) applies the s. 4(2) duties to persons who are on the premises by reason of any contract so that persons, e.g., maintaining lifts or other equipment and sub-contractors installing, e.g., central heating, may be regarded as in control and having the s. 4(2) duties. S. 4(3) also applies the duties to landlords of premises. Failure to comply with the requirements of s. 4(2) may lead to prosecution.

The duties in relation to premises will also be applicable to works sports clubs and canteens in regard to the safety of the premises and the equipment, e.g. the squash courts. The self-employed who do not themselves employ people are also affected, so that a person who runs, e.g., an amusement arcade, car wash or launderette must do what is reasonably practicable to prevent injury to persons using the premises.

The duties extend also to the employees of sub-contractors. The occupier of the premises on which they are working does not owe them duties under

s. 2 *as an employer* – though their actual employer does – but *as an occupier* and will be liable if the place of work or any equipment or material he provides is not reasonably safe. As regards the sub-contractor's employees, one can, of course, assume that they will themselves take appropriate steps as trained people to avoid the risks which are usually associated with their job.

Duties in Regard to Harmful Emissions into Atmosphere (S. 5)

S. 5(1) provides that it shall be the duty of the person having control of such premises as may be prescribed by the Secretary of State to use the best practicable means for preventing the emission into the atmosphere from the premises of noxious or offensive substances and for rendering harmless and inoffensive such substances as may be emitted. S. 53 defines 'substance' as any natural or artificial substance, whether in solid or liquid form or in the form of a gas or vapour.

It should be noted that the section is concerned only with air pollution. Pollution, e.g., by discharge of effluent into rivers is not controlled by it.

General Duties of those who Make, Import or Supply Articles of Equipment or Substances, or who Erect or Install Equipment (S. 6)

Under s. 6(1) and (4) the duties, as appropriate, are as follows –

(a) To ensure, so far as is reasonably practicable, that the article is so designed and constructed as to be safe and without risks to health when properly used, or in the case of a substance, is safe and without risks to health when properly used.

(b) To carry out or arrange for the carrying out of such testing and examination as may be necessary for the performance of the duty imposed by (a) above;

(c) To take such steps as are necessary to secure that there will be available in connection with the use of the article or substance at work adequate information about the use for which it is designed or made and has been tested, and about any conditions necessary to ensure that, when put to that use, it will be safe and without risks to health.

The definitions of articles for use at work and substances have already been given (see p. 122). As regards the definition of 'supplier', s. 53 states that where there is a reference to supplying articles or substances it means supplying them by way of sale, leasing, hire or hire purchase, whether as principal or agent for another. All forms of supply are therefore included.

As regards *installation*, and *erection* of equipment, s. 6(3) provides that it shall be the duty of any person who erects or installs any article for use at work in any premises where that article is to be used by persons at work to ensure, so far as it reasonably practicable, that nothing about the way in which it is erected or installed makes it unsafe or a risk to health when properly used.

Research, Examination and Testing (S. 6)

Under s. 6(2) and (5) it is the duty of any person who undertakes the design or manufacture of an article for use at work or the manufacture of a substance for use at work to carry out or arrange for the carrying out of any necessary research with a view to the discovery, and, so far as is reasonably practicable, the elimination or minimisation of any risks to health or safety to which the design, article or substance may give rise.

Under s. 6(6) there is no need to repeat any testing, examination or research which has been done by someone else, if it is reasonable to rely on the results of another's testing, examination or research. Thus those who lease goods are not required to go again through the manufacturer's testing, examination and research programmes.

Under s. 6(8) if you design, manufacture, import, or supply an article to somebody else's specification or request then the Act provides that if you have a *written undertaking* as part of the documentation of the contract from that person to take specified steps sufficient to ensure, so far as is reasonably practicable, that the article will be safe and without risks to health when properly used, then the written undertaking will relieve the designer, manufacturer, importer, or supplier of liability to such an extent as is reasonable, having regard to the terms of the undertaking.

General Duties of Employees at Work (S. 7)

S. 7 provides that it shall be the duty of every employee while at work —

(a) To take reasonable care for the health and safety of himself and of other persons who may be affected by his acts or omissions at work; and

(b) As regards any duty or requirement imposed on his employer or any other person by or under any of the relevant statutory provisions, to co-operate with him so far as is necessary to enable that duty or requirement to be performed or complied with.

Furthermore, s. 8 provides that no person shall intentionally or recklessly interfere with, or misuse, anything provided in the interests of health, safety or welfare.

These are useful sections which could enable an employer to enforce his safety policies. Some workers are reluctant to use safety equipment, such as machine guards, because they feel it slows them down or prevents the most efficient operation of the machine in terms of its production and of course if the employee's wages depend, because of the system of payment, upon his production, then it is even more difficult to gain his acceptance of safety devices which might affect production. In this connection it should be noted that an employee's *consent* to a dangerous practice or his connivance in it is no defence for an employer who is prosecuted under the Act.

Duty not to Charge Employees for Things Done or Provided by the Employer under the Act (S. 9)

S. 9 states that no employer shall levy or permit to be levied on any employee of his any charge in respect of anything done or provided by the employer as a result of the provisions of the Act.

The Statutory Duties and Civil Liability (S. 47)

S. 47(1)(a) provides that failure to comply with any duty imposed by ss. 2-7 or any contravention of s. 8 shall not be construed as conferring a right of action in civil proceedings.

Thus the Act creates no new civil liability. However, the ordinary action for negligence at common law remains available since s. 47(4) so provides. If there is an action by an employee at common law he can plead that the employer has been convicted under the Act, and where this is so the employee's claim is near certain to succeed.

The Health and Safety Commission and the Health and Safety Executive (SS. 10-13)

Ss. 10-13 establish the above bodies and describe their powers. In brief the Commission is concerned to make Codes of Practice, assist and encourage research and the availability of information and training, to recommend to Government areas in which new regulations are required and what they should be and, as we shall see below, to conduct inquiries.

The Executive is charged through its inspector to enforce the provisions of the Act throughout the country by covering all industries.

Investigations and Inquiries (S. 14)

If there is, e.g. a serious accident, on a particular employer's premises, then s. 14 may be brought into effect. S. 14(1) and (2) provide that whenever there has been any accident, occurrence, situation, or other matter whatsoever which the Commission thinks it necessary or expedient to investigate, which includes the situation where new regulations might be required, the Commission may —

(a) Direct the Executive to investigate the report; or

(b) Authorise another person, e.g. with particular expertise, to investigate and report; or

(c) Direct an inquiry to be held if the Secretary of State agrees.

S. 14(3) provides that normally the inquiry shall be held in public, and under s. 14(4) regulations made dealing with the conduct of inquiries may include provisions giving the person conducting the inquiry powers of entry and inspection of premises, the power to summon witnesses to give evidence or produce documents, and the power to take evidence on oath and require the making of declarations as to the truth of statements made.

S. 14(5) provides that the Commission may publish the report of the inquiry or part of it as it thinks fit.

Other Enforcement

The investigations and inquiries referred to above are, of course a form of enforcement, but in the main enforcement is through the powers conferred on the Commission and the Inspectorate.

The Commission

S. 11 gives the Commission the following general duties —

(i) To assist and encourage health and safety measures,

(ii) To make arrangements for the carrying out of research, the publication of the results of research and the provision of training and information in connection with these purposes, and to encourage provision of training and research and the publication of information by others,

(iii) To make arrangements for an information and advisory service,

(iv) To submit recommendations for new regulations,

(v) To direct the holding of investigations and inquiries.

The Inspectorate

Under ss. 21 and 22 inspectors are given power to serve improvement notices and prohibition notices.

Improvement Notice (S. 21)

S. 21 provides that if an inspector is of the opinion that a person is contravening one or more of the statutory provisions relating to health and safety or has done so in the past and the circumstances suggest he is likely to do so again, then he may serve an improvement notice on him requiring the person concerned to put matters right within the period stated in the notice.

Prohibition Notices (S. 22)

S. 22 provides that if an inspector is of the opinion that activities as they are carried on or are about to be carried on involve a risk of serious personal injury, then the inspector may serve a prohibition notice on the person who controls the activities. Under ss. 22(3) the notice must give the inspector's reasons for thinking that the activity is unsafe. When the notice has been served the activity must cease immediately. It should be noted that improvement and prohibition orders may be issued in respect of offences under the provisions of, e.g., the Factories Act, 1961 and the Offices, Shops and Railway Premises Act, 1964.

Appeal against Improvement or Prohibition Notice (S. 24)

S. 24 gives rights of appeal against improvement and prohibition notices. The appeal is to an Industrial Tribunal. An improvement notice is suspended until the appeal is heard or withdrawn and things can go on as before. A prohibition notice is not automatically suspended but may be if the person making the appeal asks for suspension and the tribunal so directs. Suspension is from the date of the direction.

There is a right of appeal from the tribunal to the Employment Appeal Tribunal both against the making of either notice or against a refusal to suspend a prohibition notice.

Power to deal with Cause of Imminent Danger (S. 25)

Under s. 25 an inspector has power to enter premises and remove from them any article which he has reasonable cause to believe is a cause of imminent danger of serious personal injury, and cause it to be made harmless, whether by destruction or in some other way. The section requires the inspector to make a report giving his reasons for taking the article and to give a copy to a responsible person at the premises from which the article was removed and to the owner if the two are not the same.

Actions against Inspectors — Indemnity (S. 26)

On general principles it is possible to bring an action for damages against an inspector who negligently issues an improvement, or more particularly, a prohibition notice. If the inspector loses his case then the Executive is given power under s. 26 to indemnify him in regard to damages, costs and expenses.

Obtaining of Information (SS. 27 and 28)

These sections carry provisions under which the Commission or the Executive can obtain information which is needed for the discharge of their duties by the serving of a notice requiring the person concerned to supply that information within a specified time.

Offences due to the Fault of Another Person (S. 36)

Under s. 36 if an offence under the Act was due to the act or default of some other person that other person is guilty of the offence and may be charged and convicted of it whether or not proceedings are taken against anyone else who is responsible.

The effect of this section is that, e.g. an executive of the company or other business organisation may be prosecuted rather than the company or other organisation where the Act was infringed because the executive himself was at fault. However, before blame can be passed on in this way the company or other organisation should have a very good system to ensure, e.g. safety, which the executive did not operate.

Offences by Bodies Corporate (S. 37)

This section also imposes potential liability upon the executive of a company but not because the executive concerned was *directly* involved in a failure to, e.g. operate a safety system under s. 36, but where the offence was committed with his *consent*, *connivance* or *neglect*.

In effect the section will enable members of boards, managers and company secretaries to be prosecuted where nothing has been done by management to prevent the commission of an offence under the Act or where with knowledge of its commission management has *consented* to, e.g. a dangerous practice being carried on or *connived* at its being carried on, as where a blind eye has been turned on the wrongful activity.

Codes of Practice

Reference has already been made to certain ACAS Codes of Practice issued under the EPCA, 1978. However, Codes of Practice may also be issued in the field of health and safety by the Health and Safety Commission. In particular, the Commission has issued a Code and Guidance Notes relating to safety committees.

Some General Matters

The Act applies to agricultural workers on farms and agricultural holdings and to employees, e.g. lorry drivers while working abroad. Part 2 of the Act is concerned with the Employment Medical Advisory Service, and in particular Para. 8 of the Third Schedule to the Act allows regulations to be made to require the making of arrangements for securing the health of persons at work or other persons, including arrangements for medical examination and health surveys.

Part 3 of the Act is concerned with building regulations and seeks to secure the health, safety, welfare and convenience of persons in or about buildings and of others who may be affected by the buildings or other matters concerned with builidngs. It is of interest mainly to builders, architects and surveyors. In particular the Act is concerned with the types of material and components used (s. 64) and this is designed in particular to have effect upon the 'towering inferno' problems which may result where certain materials are used in a building.

THE FACTORIES ACT, 1961

A Factory Defined (S. 175)

S. 175 of the Act says that the expression 'factory' means any premises in which or within the close or curtilage or precincts of which persons are employed by way of manual labour for any of the following purposes —

(i) The making of any article or part of any article, or

(ii) The altering, repairing, ornamenting, finishing, cleaning or washing, or the breaking-up, or the demolition of any article, or

(iii) The adapting for sale of any article, or

(iv) The slaughtering of cattle, sheep, swine, goats, horses, asses or mules, or

(v) The confinement of such animals as aforesaid while awaiting slaughter at other premises.

In addition the work must be carried on by way of *trade* or for the purposes of *gain* and the employer must have the right of access to, or control of, the premises.

The Act extends to premises belonging to, or in the occupation of the Crown or a local authority, even though the work may not be carried on for *gain* or by way of *trade*, though they must be premises which would be factories if they were carried on for profit. Thus a prison workshop is not a factory (*Pullen* v. *Prison Commissioners*, [1957] 2 All E.R. 470) and neither is a technical institute where instruction is given in the use of dangerous machinery (*Weston* v. *London County Council*, [1941] 1 All E.R. 555).

Manual labour

There is, of course, the requirement of *manual labour*, and in *Bound* v. *Lawrence*, [1892] 1 Q.B. 226 where a grocer's assistant was employed to serve in the shop but was occasionally engaged in manual labour in that he was required to make up parcels, it was held that the assistant was not engaged in manual labour. The case was concerned with whether the employee was a workman for the purposes of the Truck Acts (see p. 54), but it is clear from the judgment that if the issue had been whether or not the shop was a factory because of the making up of parcels, the Court would have decided that it was not.

A contrast is provided by the case of *Hoare* v. *Robert Green Ltd*, [1907] 2 K.B. 315 where it was decided that premises where flowers were made into wreaths and other floral decorations was a factory, even though the articles were sold from the same premises by the girls who made them. The girls were mainly engaged in manual labour and their workplace was a factory. The case also illustrates that the manual labour need not be heavy work.

Premises

There is normally no difficulty in deciding upon the area within which the

Act applies because the factory area is marked off by walls or fences. However, it cannot be assumed that all premises within the area are covered by the Act. For example, it was decided in *Thomas* v. *British Thompson-Houston Co. Ltd*, [1953] 1 All E.R. 29 that a building used mainly as a restaurant for administrative staff and executives was not covered by the Act, though in *Luttman* v. *Imperial Chemical Industries Ltd*, [1955] 3 All E.R. 481 the Court decided that a works canteen used for feeding and entertaining industrial workers was covered by the Act.

Safety Provisions

Some of the more important safety provisions of the 1961 Act are given below.

Fencing (S. 14)

S. 14 provides, with some exceptions, that every dangerous part of any machinery shall be securely fenced unless it is in such a position or of such construction as to be safe to persons employed or working on the premises. This provision, which was previously contained in the Factories Act of 1937, is the basis of many claims for damages by workpeople against their employers, so it is important to have at least a basic understanding of the provisions.

Dangerous parts of machinery

According to Lord Reid in *John Summers & Sons Ltd* v. *Frost*, [1955] 1 All E.R. 870 a part of machinery is dangerous if it is a *reasonably foreseeable cause* of injury to anybody acting in a way in which a human being may be reasonably expected to act in circumstances which may reasonably be expected to occur. This definition which was based on that of du Parcq, J. in *Walker* v. *Bletchley Flettons Ltd*, [1937] 1 All E.R. 170 was accepted by the House of Lords in *Close* v. *Steel Company of Wales Ltd*, [1961] 2 All E.R. 953.

Some cases illustrating the application of this foreseeability test are given below.

SMITH v. CHESTERFIELD AND DISTRICT CO-OPERATIVE SOCIETY LTD, [1953] 1 All E.R. 447: Court of Appeal

Facts

The plaintiff worked a rolling machine which rolled puff pastry. The machine was fitted with a guard to prevent the operator from having access to the rollers, though there was a 3-inch gap at the bottom of the guard. On one occasion the plaintiff, acting contrary to instructions, pushed her hand under the guard to press some dough back into the machine and was injured when her fingers came into contact with the rollers. She claimed damages from the defendants, her employers, on the basis that they were in breach of what is now s 14 of the Factories Act, 1961.

Judgment

It was held by the Court of Appeal that the conduct of the plaintiff, unreasonable as it was, was reasonably foreseeable by the defendants, and, as the guard which was provided was such that the plaintiff could put her hand beneath it and so come into contact with the rollers, the rollers of the machine were not securely fenced within the meaning of s 14 and, therefore, the defendants were in breach of their duty under that section. However, it was also held that she could not recover the whole of the damages because of her contributory negligence and the damages were in fact reduced by 60 per cent.

Comment

The case illustrates that an employer will not be absolved from liability simply because the employee is ignoring instructions, though in such a case the damages will normally be reduced on the basis of contributory negligence. In this connection the judgment of Lord Goddard, C.J. is instructive, particularly where he said: 'It has been said that the provisions of the Factories Acts regarding fencing are not meant only to prevent accidents to careful workmen. It is recognised that people in factories are not always careful, but, on the contrary, they are often thoughtless and sometimes they do things deliberately which they ought not to do and which involve themselves in injury. Fencing is intended to protect the careless and the ignorant as well as the careful and the well-instructed.'

JOHN SUMMERS & SONS LTD v. FROST, [1955] 1 All E.R. 870: House of Lords

Facts

Mr Frost was employed by Summers as a maintenance fitter. He was grinding some metal on a power-driven grinding wheel when his thumb came into contact with the wheel and he was injured. The machine was fitted with an efficient hood which left only an arc of 7 inches of the stone exposed for the purposes of access.

Judgment

It was held by the House of Lords that the grinding stone was a dangerous part of the machine within s 14 so that there was an absolute obligation that it should be securely fenced to prevent reasonably foreseeable injury regardless of whether those using the machine were careless or inattentive. The machine was, therefore, not securely fenced and Summers were in breach of their duty under s 14, even though it was accepted that the grinding machine could not be securely fenced in terms of s 14 except by a hood which would render it commercially unuseable.

Comment

It should be noted that where a machine is rendered unuseable if it is securely fenced in terms of s 14, regulations permitting a more restricted form of fencing may be made under s 60 of the 1961 Act.

In discussing the nature of the employer's duty under s 14, Lord Simonds said in *Nicholls* v. *Austin (Leyton) Ltd*, [1946] 2 All E.R. 92 that: 'The danger to be guarded against is in the contact of worker with machine.' It was held in *Nicholls* that s 14 imposed no duty to fence against a workman being struck by a piece of wood flying out of a woodworking machine. Furthermore, it has been held that there is no breach of statutory duty where broken parts of machinery or tools are ejected while it is in motion (see *Carroll* v. *Andrew Barclay & Sons Ltd*, [1948] 2 All E.R. 386 and *Close* v. *Steel Company of Wales Ltd*, [1961] 2 All E.R. 953). However, each case depends very much upon its own facts and in *Wearing* v. *Pirelli Ltd*, [1977] 1 All E.R. 339 the House of Lords held that s 14 had been infringed where the plaintiff's hand had come into contact with an unfenced revolving drum used in the production of motor tyres, even though the injury was caused by contact with rubber fabric covering the revolving drum and not with the drum itself. The House of Lords distinguished *Nicholls* and said that if one looked at the whole incident in a practical way, the injury had been caused by the revolving drum and accordingly the defendants were liable to the plaintiff for their breach of statutory duty.

Before leaving the topic of dangerous parts of machinery the case of *Millard* v. *Serck Tubes Ltd* (see below) should be noted. According to the Court of Appeal in that case the foreseeability test goes only to deciding whether or not a machine should be fenced in the first place. If it is dangerous enough to require a proper fence under the foreseeability test and it does not have such a fence then there is a breach of s 14 and the employer is liable for injuries which occur, even though the circumstances are unusal.

MILLARD v. SERCK TUBES LTD, [1969] 1 All E.R. 598: Court of Appeal

Facts

The plaintiff operated a power drill during the course of his employment. The drill had a fence but the guard was not complete in that there was a gap in it through which the operator's hand could be drawn. While the plaintiff's hand was resting on the guard a piece of swarf, which is metal strip, was thrown out from the drill and wound itself around the plaintiff's hand and drew it into the drill causing him injury. The defendant employers conceded that the drill was not properly fenced contrary to s 14 of the 1961 Act but at first instance Faulks, J. had dismissed the plaintiff's application on the ground that the injury was caused in a way that was not reasonably foreseeable.

Judgment

The Court of Appeal held that the plaintiff's appeal be allowed. If a workman in a factory is injured, the Court decided, by a dangerous part of machinery which is not securely fenced as required by s 14 of the 1961 Act, and if the injury would not have occurred had that part been fenced as required by the Act, the occupier of the factory is liable in damages to the workman for breach of statutory duty, even though the accident occurs in an entirely unforeseeable way.

Comment

It should be noted that the Court of Appeal distinguished *Close* v. *Steel Company of Wales Ltd*, (1961), to which reference has been made, saying that that case was relevant only where a person had been injured by a component flying out of a machine or by some part of the machine itself flying out.

Exceptions to fencing requirements (ss 15 and 16)

Under s 15 of the Act the fencing provisions do not apply where a machine is being *examined*, *lubricated* or *adjusted* while in motion in circumstances where the work can only be done while the machine is in motion, provided that the work is carried out by a person over the age of 18 years.

Furthermore, under s 16 the statutory provisions regarding fencing apply only if the machine concerned is *in motion or use*. This would appear to mean when the machine is in motion during the ordinary course of its work. Certainly, not every form of movement is covered.

Thus in *Richard Thomas & Baldwins, Ltd* v. *Cummings* [1955] 1 All E.R. 285, Cummings was adjusting a machine which, when working, was driven by belts passing over pulleys. The power had been cut off while Cummings made the adjustment and the covers over the pulleys and belts had been removed. In order to make the adjustments Cummings rotated the machine by pulling the belt by hand and was injured during this process. His employers admitted that when the machine was in use it should be fenced but suggested that this was not the case where, as here, the machine had been disconnected from motive power. The House of Lords agreed with the employers and Cummings' claim that they were in breach of their duty to fence failed. 'The words "in motion or in use" in section 16 do not, in my opinion, refer to such movement of machinery by hand as took place in the present case, and section 16 does not deal in any way with such movements.' (per Lord Oaksey.)

It should be noted that what is said above relates only to a claim for breach of statutory duty. An employer who is found not to have infringed the Factories Act may still be liable at common law for allowing an unsafe system of work to operate.

Floor, passages and stairs (s 28)

Under s 28 all floors, stairs, passages and gangways must be of sound construction, properly maintained and, so far as is reasonably practicable, kept free from any obstruction and free from any substance which is likely to cause persons to slip. A number of cases have been brought under this section; the two which follow provide some illustration of its application.

DORMAN LONG (STEEL) v. BELL, [1964] 1 All E.R. 617:
House of Lords

Facts

Two heavy metal plates were put temporarily on the floor of a factory with one end propped up. The plates became slippery when a layer of slag dust collected on them and Mr Bell, who was employed on maintenance work at night, stepped on them whilst making his way to the place where he had to work. He slipped off the plates, injured himself, and sued Dorman's, his employers, for damages based on a breach of s 28 of the Act of 1961.

Judgment

It was held by the House of Lords that Mr Bell's action succeeded, notwithstanding that the slippery slag dust was not in direct contact with the floor.

LATIMER v. A.E.C. Ltd, [1953] 2 All E.R. 449: House of Lords

Facts

Mr Latimer was a milling machine operator employed by A.E.C. at their works in Southall, Middlesex. The works were about 15 acres in extent and some 4000 people were employed there. Because of an extraordinarily heavy rainstorm the factory became flooded and the flood water mixed with oil used for cooling the machines. When the water had drained away there was a slippery film of oil left on the surface of the floor. The employer spread sawdust on the floor but, because a very large area was involved and the flood was unprecedented, there was not enough sawdust to cover the whole floor. Mr Latimer slipped on part of the floor which was not treated and was injured. He then brought a claim for damages against his employers for a breach of s 28 of the Factories Act, 1961.

Judgment

It was held by the House of Lords that the employers were not in breach of their statutory duty under s 28. The section was concerned with the general condition and soundness of construction of the floor and did not relate to what the Court referred to as a 'transient and exceptional condition'. In addition, the employers had taken every reasonable step to avoid danger and were not liable for negligence at common law either.

Comment

In *Latimer's case* the employer seems to have done all that was reasonably possible. In *Bell* the employer also raised an argument that it was not reasonably practicable to keep the floor clear but in that case evidence showed that no attempt had been made to remove the plates from the floor and the House of Lords felt that on the facts it was reasonably practicable to have removed them.

THE OFFICES, SHOPS AND RAILWAY PREMISES ACT, 1963

The provisions relating to railway premises are not of major importance and this part of the book will be confined to offices and shops.

Offices and Shops Defined (S 1)

S 1 gives lengthy definitions of premises to which the Act applies but briefly, *office premises* includes a builidng or part of a building, the sole or principal use of which is for *office purposes*. The expression 'office purposes' includes the functions of administration, handling of money, telephone and telegraph operating and clerical work, such as writing, book keeping, filing, sorting papers, typing, duplicating, machine calculating, drawing and the preparation of material for publication. Premises used in conjunction are also included, such as dining rooms, wash rooms, strong rooms, storage rooms, and approaches and exits.

As regards *shop premises*, these include shops in the usual sense of the word and also all buildings or parts of them which are used for the retail trade, warehouses in the occupation of wholesalers, buildings at which the public is invited to deliver goods for repair or other treatment and open fuel storage premises such as coal depots. There are some exceptions, notably, premises where no-one is employed except the husband, wife, parent, grandparent, son, daughter, grandchild, brother or sister of the employer (s 2). This, of course, exempts many retail shops run by families.

Health, Safety and Welfare Provisions

Under s 4 all premises, furniture, furnishings and fittings must be kept clean. In addition, under s 5, rooms in which people work must not be overcrowded, and under s 6 effective provision must be made for securing and maintaining a reasonable temperature in rooms where persons are employed other than for short periods. If the work being done does not involve serious physical effort a temperature of not less than 16°C (60.80°F) after the first hour is reasonable. The Act also requires that a thermometer be provided in a conspicuous place on each floor of the premises.

There are some exceptions such as rooms in which goods are stored which would deteriorate at 16°C. However, employees who work in such rooms must be provided with convenient, accessible and effective means of warming themselves.

S 7 provides that every room in which persons are employed shall be adequately ventilated and supplied with fresh or artificially purified air, and under s 8 there must be suitable and sufficient lighting, either natural or artificial, in all parts of the premises.

Under s 9 suitable and sufficient sanitary conveniences must be provided. These must be kept clean and be properly maintained, lit and ventilated. Regulations made under the Act provide that where there are male and female employees separate lavatories shall be provided for each sex.

Under s 10 suitable and sufficient washing facilities must be provided. This includes a supply of clean, running, hot and cold or warm water, soap and clean towels or other suitable means of drying.

S 11 requires that an adequate supply of wholesome drinking water be made available. If the supply is not piped it must be contained in suitable vessels and must be renewed daily. If water is supplied other than by jet, a supply of disposable drinking vessels must be available and, if washable, non-disposable vessels are used there must be a supply of clean water in which to rinse them.

Under s 12 suitable and sufficient provisions must be made for clothing which is not worn while at work and so far as is reasonably practicable arrangements must be made for drying the clothing.

Where reasonable opportunities exist for sitting during working hours, s 13 provides that suitable sitting facilities are to be made available, and under s 14 those who sit to do their work must obviously be provided with a seat together with a foot rest if, e.g., an employee is short-legged and cannot support his or her feet comfortably without one.

As regards floors, passages and stairs, these must, under s 16, be of sound construction, properly maintained and kept free from obstruction and slippery substances. Handrails must be provided on stairways and where a stairway is open on both sides there must be two handrails and both sides must be guarded to prevent persons slipping between the rails and the steps. In addition, all openings in floors must be fenced except insofar as the nature of the work makes such fencing impracticable.

As regards fencing of machinery, s 17 provides that dangerous parts of machinery must be fenced unless the machine is as safe without a fence as it would be with one.

By s 18 no person under 18 may clean any machinery if this exposes him to risk of injury and s 19 provides that no person shall work dangerous machinery unless he or she has received sufficient training or is under adequate supervision by a person with thorough knowledge and experience of the machine.

Finally, under s 20, the Secretary of State may make regulations to secure safety in special classes of buildings or processes and may prohibit the use of machinery considered dangerous.

S 23 deals with heavy work and provides that persons shall not be required to lift, carry or move loads which are so heavy as to be likely to cause injury to them.

S 24 deals with first-aid provisions and states that all premises to which the Act applies must have a first-aid box or cupboard readily accessible and containing only first-aid requisites or appliances. Where there are more than 150 workers there must be one box for each 150 workers or fraction thereof.

slipper

As regards fires, s 28 states that all premises covered by the Act must be provided with such means of escape in case of fire as may reasonably be required in view of, e.g. the number of employees *and* other persons who may be expected to be on the premises. Under s 30 all means of escape must be properly maintained and kept free from obstruction. S 33 deals with exits and states that all doors must be capable of being opened immediately if persons are working or eating on the premises and all exits must be clearly marked as such. S 34 requires the fitting of an adequate alarm system and for it to be tested at least every three months. S 36 requires in effect a system of fire drill so that persons employed know the means of escape and the routine to be followed if fire breaks out. Finally, s 38 requires the provision and maintenance of fire-fighting equipment which is readily available for use.

6 Employer's Liability for Injuries to his Employee

Although National Insurance legislation provides for benefits to be payable to those injured in the course of employment (see p. 153) there are still many instances where an employee who is injured at work will wish to sue his employer for damages at common law. In this connection it is worth noting that an employer *must insure* himself in respect of vicarious liability for injuries caused by his employees to their colleagues, though insurance is not compulsory in respect of injuries caused to persons who are not employees.

These common law claims are brought on the basis of negligence by the employer and, because of the decision of the House of Lords in *Wilsons and Clyde Coal Co.* v. *English*, [1938] A.C. 57, the duty of care which an employer owes to his employee at common law is usually considered under the headings which appear below.

FELLOW EMPLOYEES

An employer is under a duty to select fellow employees who will not injure their colleagues and he can be liable for damage caused by his failure to do so. This duty applies, of course, to incompetent employees whose negligence causes injury, but the duty has extended to injury caused by other forms of conduct.

> **VENESS v. DYSON, BELL & CO.,** *The Times*, 25 May 1965:
> **High Court**
>
> **Facts**
>
> The plaintiff claimed damages against her former employers alleging that bullying and persecution by fellow-employees had brought her to the point of a nervous breakdown. She further alleged that the employers should have provided reasonable conditions under which she could carry out her duties and should have taken reasonable steps to protect her from interference by her colleagues and that they had failed to exercise due skill and care in maintaining proper discipline. The employers said that these allegations did not disclose a cause of action on which to proceed to trial.

Judgment

It was held by Widgery, J. that the allegations should not be struck out. The matter should proceed to trial to see if the allegations could be proved.

SAFE PLANT APPLIANCES AND PREMISES

This involves a duty both to *provide* and *maintain* suitable plant.

LOVELL v. BLUNDELLS AND CROMPTON & CO. LTD, [1944] 2 All E.R. High Court

Facts

Lovell was told by the defendants who were his employers to carry out an overhaul of a ship's boiler tubes. He could not reach certain of the tubes so he procured some planks for himself and from them made up his own staging. The planks were unsound and collapsed, injuring Lovell. The defendants had not provided any form of staging nor had they laid down any system of working.

Judgment

Mr Justice Tucker held that the employers were liable in negligence. They had failed to supply plant in a situation where there was an obvious requirement for it.

BAKER v. JAMES BROS & SONS LTD, [1921] 2 K.B. 674: High Court

Facts

Baker, who was a commercial traveller employed by the defendants, had to travel in a particular district taking orders and for this purpose the defendants supplied him with a car. The starting gear was defective and Baker complained to the defendants several times about this but nothing was done. One one occasion while Baker was out taking orders he was badly injured while trying to start the car.

Judgment

The Court held that Baker was entitled to damages. His employers had failed to maintain the car as they should. In the circumstances Baker could not be regarded as having consented to run the risk of injury, nor could he be regarded as guilty of contributory negligence.

In this connection the Employer's Liability (Defective Equipment) Act, 1969 imposes strict liability on an employer who provides defective equipment which causes injury to an employee. If the defect is wholly or partly due to the fault of the manufacturer then the employer is still liable but may recover any damages he has had to pay his employee from the manufacturer, and where, for example, the manufacturer has more money than the employer, the injured employee can sue the manufacturer direct.

As regards *premises*, an employer must exercise reasonable care to ensure that his *own premises and the place of work* are safe. The duty also extends to the premises of a third party.

M'QUILTER v. GOULANDRIS BROS LTD, [1951] S.L.T. (Notes) 75: Court of Session

Facts

In this Scottish case employees who were repairing a ship had to walk along an unlighted deck. One employee caught his foot in a ring-bolt and was killed when he tripped into an uncovered hatch.

Judgment

His employers were held liable in negligence. They should at the very least have provided some form of lighting.

In the course of his judgment Lord Guthrie said: 'The fact that the work had to be carried out on the premises of a third party did not absolve an employer from his duty of exercising reasonable care for the safety of his workmen. The duty must still be fulfilled, although its scope is circumscribed by the fact that the work was being done on premises not within the possession and control of the employer. As the structure of the premises is outwith his control, and any defects therein beyond his power to rectify, his care for his men could only be exercised within the limits imposed by those circumstances. But he was still under the duty of exercising reasonable care to safeguard them against dangers which he should anticipate and which he had power to avert.'

There are, of course, statutory duties relating to safe premises (see p. 122), but neither the statutory nor the common law duties are absolute and are not broken if the workplace becomes unsafe because of something exceptional or transient (see *Latimer* v. *A.E.C. Ltd*, (1953) p. 138).

SAFE SYSTEM OF WORK

An employer is required to set up and enforce a safe system of working, and in this connection Lord Greene, M.R. said in *Speed* v. *Swift (Thomas) & Co. Ltd,* [1943] 1 All E.R. 549; Court of Appeal: 'I do not venture to suggest a definition of what is meant by system. But it ... may include ... the physical lay-out of the job — the setting of the stage, so to speak — the sequence in which the work is to be carried out, the provision in proper cases of warnings and notices and the issue of special instructions. A system may be adequate for the whole course of the job or it may have to be modified or improved to meet circumstances which arise; such modifications or improvements appear to me equally to fall under the head of system.'

The system must take account of the fact that *employees may, as a result of inexperience or over-confidence, be careless* about the risks involved in their work. In addition, the system must be adequate to protect employees *with known infirmities.*

GENERAL CLEANING CONTRACTORS LTD v. CHRISTMAS, [1952] 2 All E.R. 1110: House of Lords

Facts

Christmas was an experienced window cleaner. He was engaged in cleaning windows at the Caledonian Club in London. His employers provided safety belts but the club's premises had no fittings to which belts could be attached. Christmas carried out the work by getting hand- and footholds from window frames and sills. A defective sash allowed a window to drop on his hand. He lost his hold and fell, suffering injuries.

Judgment

The House of Lords held that the employers were liable. They should have provided wedges to keep sashes from closing. The system of work was unsafe.

'It is ... well known to employers ... that their workpeople are very frequently, if not habitually, careless about the risks which their work may involve.' (per Lord Oaksey.)

PARIS v. STEPNEY BOROUGH COUNCIL, [1951] A.C. 367: House of Lords

Facts

The defendants employed Paris on vehicle maintenance. The defendants knew that he had the use of only one eye. While in the course of his duties Paris was struck in his good eye by a chip of metal and became totally blind. He sued the defendants in negligence, saying that they should have provided him with goggles, although it was not usual practice as regards men with two good eyes.

Judgment

The House of Lords held the employers liable. It might not be necessary to provide goggles for normal workmen but it was for a one-eyed workman. Total blindness was a much more serious risk than the loss of one eye.

'There are occupations in which the possibility of an accident occurring to a workman is extremely remote, while there are other occupations in which there is constant risk of accident. Similarly, there are occupations in which, if an accident occurs, it is likely to be of a trivial nature, whilst there are other occupations in which . . . the result . . . may well be fatal . . . there is in each case a gradually ascending scale between the two extremes . . . the more serious the damage which will happen if an accident occurs, the more thorough are the precautions which an employer must take.' (per Lord Morton.)

It is also the duty of the employer to enforce a safe system having once set it up, though an employer may rely upon an experienced worker being sensible enough to abide by the system.

WOODS v. DURABLE SUITES, [1953] 2 All E.R. 391: Court of Appeal

Facts

The defendants used synthetic glue in their veneer department. The use of the glue created a risk of dermatitis in employees. The defendants instructed their employees in the use of a barrier cream soap to prevent dermatitis. They also posted a notice near the workplace setting out the precautions to be taken and provided washing facilities. Woods was 56 years of age and an experienced workman but, unknown to his employers, he never fully observed the precautionary procedures. He contracted dermatitis and sued his employers for negligence.

Judgment

The Court of Appeal held that the employers were not liable. They could not be expected to keep mature and experienced employees under constant supervision to see that they obeyed instructions.

The workman who is injured must prove that a failure of the system actually caused his injuries.

McWILLIAMS v. SIR WILLIAM ARROL & CO. LTD, [1962] 1 All E.R. 623: House of Lords

Facts

The plaintiff's husband, a steel erector, was killed by a fall from a steel tower on which he was working. There was a statutory duty on the employer under the Factories Act, 1936 (applicable in Scotland) to supply safety belts. The belts had been withdrawn from the site but the employers adduced evidence to show that the plaintiff's husband would not have worn a belt even if one had been available.

Judgment

The House of Lords held that the plaintiff's action failed. She had established a breach of duty but not causation.

'If I prove that my breach of duty in no way caused or contributed to the accident I cannot be liable in damages. And if the accident would have happened in just the same way whether or not I fulfilled my duty, it is obvious that my failure to fulfil my duty cannot have caused or contributed to it.' (per Lord Reid.)

'On the second submission, that the (defendants) should have exhorted or instructed the deceased to use a safety belt, I have considered carefully the argument based on the extent of the danger. I have, however, come to the conclusion that it fails. There was a strong feeling among steel erectors that safety belts were certainly cumbersome and might be dangerous except in very special circumstances which did not obtain here . . . ' (per Viscount Kilmuir, L.C.)

However, a worker may be assisted in his burden of proof where the maxim *res ipsa loquitur* applies. Although the burden of proof in negligence normally lies on the plaintiff, there is a principle known as *res ipsa loquitur* (the thing speaks for itself) and where the principle applies the court is prepared to lighten the plaintiff's burden. In some cases it is difficult for the plaintiff to show how much care the defendant has taken and it is a commonsense rule of evidence to allow the plaintiff to prove the result and not require him to prove any particular act or omission by the defendant. Before the principle can apply the thing causing the damage must be shown to be under the control of the defendant, and the accident which happened must be one which does not normally occur unless negligence is present. On proof of this situation negligence in the defendant will be assumed, and he will be liable unless he can explain the occurrence on grounds other than his negligence. The explanation must, of course, be convincing to the court, and it is not enough to offer purely hypothetical explanations.

An illustration of the use of the maxim in an employment situation is provided by the following case.

MOORE v. R. FOX & SONS, [1956] 1 All E.R. 182: Court of Appeal

Facts

Moore's job was to remove rust from metal objects by immersing them in a tank filled with liquid chemicals. The chemicals had to be kept at a temperature of 140°F. A gas burner beneath the tank provided the heat. It was automatic and thermostatically controlled and not in any sense under Moore's control. Moore was killed by an explosion under the tank and Mrs Moore claimed damages from his employers.

Judgment

The Court held that Mrs Moore was entitled to damages. The maxim *res ipsa loquitur* applied. The burner was under the management of the employer and the accident would not have happened if proper care had been taken.

DEFENCES AVAILABLE TO EMPLOYER

An employer who is in breach of his duty of care may nevertheless be able to raise certain defences to a claim by his employee. These are set out below.

Contributory Negligence

This defence was considered more fully in Chapter 1 (see p. 17), and it is only necessary here to note that contributory negligence is available as a defence to an employer in an action brought against him by an employee who alleges injury as a result of his employer's negligence.

The defence is available in claims based on common law negligence and on breach of statutory duty. Thus in *Cakebread* v. *Hopping Brothers (Whetstone) Ltd*, [1947] 1 All E.R. 389: Court of Appeal, the employers of the plaintiff who was engaged in a woodworking factory had failed to see that the guard on a circular saw was properly adjusted and the plaintiff, who worked the saw, was injured as a result. However, it appeared that the plaintiff did not like working the machine with the guard properly adjusted and he had arranged with his foreman that the saw should be operated with an improperly adjusted guard. It was held that the employer was in breach of his common law duty of care and also of a statutory duty under the Woodworking Machinery Regulations, 1922. However, the Court of Appeal found that the plaintiff had failed to exercise the care of a prudent man for his own safety and reduced his damages by 50%.

Assumption of Risk by Employee

The defence of *volenti non fit injuria*, as this defence is otherwise called, was considered more fully in Chapter 1 (see p. 15). It is unlikely to provide a successful defence these days since it is now well established that an employee who *knows* of a risk cannot for that reason be regarded as having *consented* to take it.

SMITH v. BAKER & SONS, [1891] A.C. 325; House of Lords

Facts

Smith was employed by Baker & Sons to drill holes in some rock in a railway cutting. A crane, operated by fellow employees, often swung heavy stones over Smith's head while he was working on the rock face. Both Smith and his employers realised that there was a risk that the stones might fall, but the crane was nevertheless operated without any warning being given at the moment of jibbing or swinging. Smith was injured by a stone which fell from the crane because of negligent strapping of the load.

Judgment

The House of Lords held that Smith had not voluntarily undertaken the risk of his employers' negligence and that his knowledge of the danger did not prevent his recovering damages.

The defence is not available to an employer who is in breach of a *statutory duty laid upon him*. (*Wheeler* v. *New Merton Board Mills Ltd*, [1933] 2 K.B. 669.)

However, it may be raised as a defence by an employer who has become vicariously liable for a *breach of statutory duty laid upon one of his employees*.

IMPERIAL CHEMICAL INDUSTRIES LTD v. SHATWELL, [1964] 2 All E.R. 999: House of Lords

Facts

George and James Shatwell were certified and experienced shotfirers employed by I.C.I. Statutory rules imposed an obligation on them personally (not on their employers) to ensure that certain operations connected with shotfiring should not be done unless all persons in the vicinity had taken cover. They knew of the risks of premature explosion which had been explained to them; they knew of the prohibition; but on one occasion because a cable they had was too short to reach the shelter they decided to test without taking cover rather than wait ten minutes for their companion, Beswick, who had gone to fetch a longer cable. James gave George two wires, and George applied them to the galvanometer terminals. An explosion occurred and both men were injured.

Judgment

At the trial it was found that James was guilty of negligence and breach of statutory duty for which the employers were held vicariously liable, damages being assessed at £1500 on a basis of 50 per cent contributory negligence. The Court of Appeal affirmed, but the House of Lords *reversed*, the decision and held that, although James's acts were a contributory cause of the accident to George, the employers were not liable, because —

(a) They were not themselves in breach of a statutory duty.
(b) They could plead *volenti non fit injuria* to a claim of vicarious liability.
(c) They had shown no negligence. They had instilled the need for caution, made proper provision, and even arranged a scale of remuneration in a way which removed a temptation to take short cuts.
(d) The Shatwell brothers were trained men well aware of the risk involved, so the principle of *volenti non fit injuria* applied. Lord Pearce said: 'The defence [of *volenti non fit injuria*] should be available where the employer was not in breach of a statutory duty and was not vicariously in breach of a statutory duty through the neglect of some person of superior rank to the plaintiff and whose commands the plaintiff was bound to obey or who has some special and different duty of care.'

Comment

If the employers had been compelled to rely on the defence of contributory negligence, they might have escaped liability if only one man were involved and treated as solely responsible. However, where two men were involved, as here, they would have been vicariously liable for James's contribution to George's injury and for George's contribution to James's injury, so they would have been compelled to partially compensate each man.

FATAL ACCIDENTS

If as a result of the employer's negligence, an employee is killed in the course of employment there are two sorts of claim against the employer which are set out below.

Claim by the Estate of the Deceased Employee

Under the Law Reform (Miscellaneous Provisions) Act, 1934 all causes of action in tort (other than defamation) subsisting at the time of a person's death survive for or against his estate.

Thus the personal representatives of the deceased employee can sue the employer for damages. However, damages recoverable by the estate of the deceased in regard to loss of expectation of life are not large. This arises from *Benham* v. *Gambling*, [1941] A.C. 157, where the House of Lords held that the amount recoverable is not to be affected by the wealth of the deceased, nor his prospects of future earnings, nor his views as to his future happiness, but by the happiness he might in fact enjoy. Their Lordships awarded £200 in this case, but in more recent cases the court has taken into account the fall in the value of money and higher awards have been made. Even so, in *Dodds* v. *Dodds, The Times*, 29 July 1977, Balcombe, J. in considering the death of Mr Dodds by reason of the negligence of another, awarded only £913 to the estate under the 1934 Act but some £17,168 to a dependent son aged 12 under the Fatal Accidents Act (see below).

Claims by Dependents of Deceased Employee

Under the provisions of the Fatal Accidents Act, 1976 an employer whose negligence has caused the death of an employee may be liable to certain relatives of the employee who have suffered financial loss because of the death, though damages recoverable by such dependants under the 1976 Act will be reduced by any sums awarded to the employee's estate under the 1934 Act if the estate has devolved on those dependents under a will or on intestacy as where the employee dies without leaving a will. The following persons are entitled to claim if they were dependent on the deceased; husband, wife (but not a divorced wife or the so-called common-law wife), children, grandchildren, parents, grandparents, brothers, sisters, aunts and uncles, and their issue; the relationship may be traced through step-relatives, adoption or illegitimacy, and relatives by marriage have the same rights as the deceased's own relatives.

A single action must be brought on behalf of all eligible dependents and the total damages apportioned according to their dependancy. The action may be brought by the personal representatives of the deceased, but if there are none, or if they fail to bring the action within six months from the death, the dependents may bring it. The action is barred if it is not brought within three years of the death which is the subject of the claim.

If the deceased was guilty of contributory negligence or was a volunteer the damages awarded to dependents will be reduced or extinguished according to the degree to which the deceased was at fault or was a volunteer.

The probability of pecuniary loss is a matter for the plaintiff to prove, and the court to decide as a matter of fact. However, it should be noted that the object of the Fatal Accidents Act is to provide *maintenance* for relatives who have been deprived of maintenance by the death. Therefore, if the relative seeking to claim is already adequately provided for from some other source, he will not be able to claim under these provisions. Damages awarded are not, however, to be reduced on account of any insurance money, National Insurance or friendly society or trade union benefit, pension, or gratuity accruing to a relative, even though the pecuniary loss is thereby reduced.

7 Employment and Social Security

This is a complex area of the law, and the treatment given to it here is by intention environmental. It is not necessary for the non-specialist to have more than a basic knowledge of the principles involved. For the smaller firm there are Departments of State ready and willing to advise as to details and larger organisations will normally have their own specialists operating, e.g. within the personnel function.

INDUSTRIAL INJURIES

A system of industrial injury benefit is operated by the State. It is financed by contributions from employers and employees and from money provided by Parliament. The current legislation is contained in the Social Security Act, 1975, though legal decisions based on earlier and similar legislation which commenced with the Workmen's Compensation Act, 1897 provide many of the illustrations.

Risks Covered

Benefit is available to an insured person who suffers *personal injury* by reason of an *accident* arising *out of* and *in the course of* his employment (s. 50(1)), and also where he contracts any *prescribed disease* or *personal injury* which is not the result of an accident but is due to the nature of the employment (s. 76(1)).

Personal Injury

This expression extends to mental injury arising, e.g. from shock, but damage to the property of an insured person is not covered. Thus in a claim made in 1956 it was held that damage to an artificial leg was not admissible to claim as an industrial injury (R (I) 5/56).

Accident

We generally think of injuries from accidents as being caused by, e.g. falling or tripping, or being struck by something. However, 'accident' was defined by Lord Shand in *Fenton* v. *Thorley*, [1903] A.C. 443 as 'any unexpected personal injury resulting to the workman in the course of his employment from any unlooked-for mishap or occurrence'. In the case the House of Lords held that rupture by over-exertion when turning a wheel was an accident.

An accident must, however, be distinguished from a disease. By 'disease' is meant a situation of slowly deteriorating health brought on by an industrial process.

Industrial diseases also attract State benefits if they are *prescribed*. At the time of writing there are some 50 prescribed diseases and further information as to these is available from the Department of Health and Social Security. In addition, there is special legislation for pneumoconiosis, byssinosis, or diffuse mesotheliomia (see Pneumoconiosis, etc. (Workers' Compensation) Act, 1979).

A claimant's state of health at the time when the accident occurred is not relevant provided there has been an accident. Thus it has been held that angina pectoris resulting from the lifting of heavy weights was injury by accident although the claimant already had a heart disease (C.I. 27/49).

Deliberate harm is also included so that in one case a claimant recovered benefit when he suffered scalding because his employer's daughter-in-law, with whom he worked, threw boiling water over him (C.I. 51/49).

Course of Employment

As we have seen, the accident must arise *out of* and *in the course of* employment. This is a matter of *fact* for the court to decide, but in general terms accidents during the contractual period between starting and finishing work will be covered, plus a reasonable time at the beginning and end of such period when the worker is on his employer's premises, going to or leaving the workplace.

DAVIDSON & CO. v. M'ROBB, [1918] A.C. 304: House of Lords

Facts

A ship's chief engineer went ashore for his own purposes. He returned to the ship in the dark, fell from the quay and drowned.

Judgment

The claim for compensation failed because the engineer left the ship for his own purposes, i.e. shore leave, and that was an interruption of his employment.

'The word "employment" must mean the same thing when in apposition with "in the course of" — as it means when in apposition with "out of". "Arising out of the employment" obviously means arising out of the work which the man is employed to do and which is incident to it — in other words, out of his service. "In the course of the employment" must mean, similarly, in the course of the work which the man is employed to do, and what is incident to it — in other words, in the course of his service. In the case of a domestic servant who sleeps and takes his meals in his master's house he is in the course of his service all the time — his service is interrupted if he goes out on his own business or pleasure. A workman who by the terms of his employment takes his meals on his employer's premises is in the course of his service in being there at meal times. In either case the master or employer would be liable for damages caused by such an accident ... as it would arise out of the employment, an incident of which is the presence of the servant or workman upon the premises when partaking of his meals; but different considerations might apply if the injury proceeded from choking over a morsel of food, as the act of eating may be no part of the service.

'The words "and in the course of" were probably added for this reason. If the nerve or agility of a workman were impaired by the conditions of his work, and in consequence he met with an accident in the street which he would have avoided but for the impairment of his health occasioned by his work, the accident might be said to arise "out of the employment". The same thing might be said in the case of an accident which he would have escaped but for the fatigue induced by working overtime. The introduction of such claims is prevented by the words "in the course of the employment". Such an accident as above suggested, though it might arise out of the work, would not be in the course of the work. "In the course of the employment" does not mean during the currency of the time of the engagement. If the words meant this they would be useless, and would add nothing to the words "arising out of the employment", while to interpret them in this sense would let in the possibility of a number of claims of the nature above indicated, which the words "in the course of the employment" rightly read as meaning in the course of the work or service would exclude. If "in the course of the employment" meant during the currency of the engagement, a sailor engaged for a round voyage would be in the course of his employment while in a public-house in any port where he had leave to go on shore. "Course" is more applicable to work or service than to the currency of the engagement. Leave on shore on the sailor's own business or pleasure is an interruption of his employment, not in the course of it.' (per Lord Finlay.)

However, activities reasonably incidental to work are regarded as in the course of employment.

KNIGHT v. HOWARD WALL LTD, [1938] 4 All E.R. 667: Court of Appeal

Facts

Knight suffered an eye injury when a dart flew off a dart board. This happened in the works canteen when he was eating his lunch. Employees were not bound to use the canteen but could do so if they wished. Knight claimed compensation.

Judgment

The Court of Appeal held that he was entitled to compensation because the accident arose out of and in the course of his employment.

'The facts of the present case are these. There were provided, either by the employer or by the contractor, facilities for playing darts. An ill-directed dart may prove an extremely dangerous instrument, being in its nature rather like an arrow, with a sharp pointed end. If this man had been required to go into that room, where darts were admittedly being played, and where a dart might strike against a wall, or might without negligence strike a person — because it is not to be assumed that everybody who plays darts has the accuracy of William Tell in dealing with these things — and if his duty had been to do a specific piece of work such as paint the wall, it could not possibly be disputed that there would be evidence that his employment had brought him into a place where he was exposed to danger — namely, the danger of these sharp instruments, which, to the employers' knowledge, were being habitually thrown about this room. Can it make any difference that he is there in the course of his employment, as a term of the contract which gives him a right to be there, rather than in the carrying out of a duty? I think that it can make none. Once it is established that it is part of the course of the employment — that is to say, that it is a term of his contract that he should be there — the accident which arises at that point, if the place is one where there is a specific danger, is one which, I think, arises out of the employment.' (per Slesser, L.J.)

In this connection it should be noted that s. 50(3) of the Social Security Act, 1975 provides that an accident arising in the course of a worker's employment shall be deemed also to have arisen out of that employment unless there is evidence to the contrary.

Thus there is a *presumption* that where an accident arose in the course of employment, it arose out of it and so benefit is payable. This presumption obviously assists the worker in making his claim because the insurance officer has to prove that benefit is not payable.

Acts in Breach of Regulations

Under s. 52 of the 1975 Act an accident is deemed to arise out of and in the course of employment, even though the worker is at the time of the accident acting in contravention of any statutory or other regulations applicable to his employment or of any orders given by or on behalf of his employer or that he is acting without instructions from his employer if —

(a)   the accident would have been deemed to have arisen out of and in the course of employment had there been no contravention, and

(b)   the act was done for the purpose of and in connection with the employer's trade or business.

Thus if a worker is injured acting within the scope of his employment he will be entitled to benefit even if he is disobeying orders or has not been told to do what he is doing. This is illustrated by a case in which a miner who, against statutory regulations, rode on a coal tub which he was employed to drive and not to ride on, and was injured, was held entitled to benefit because he was doing what he was employed to do even though in a forbidden way (C.I. 11/49).

Travelling in Employer's Transport

S. 53 of the 1975 Act provides that an accident happening while a worker is, with the express or implied permission of his employer, travelling as a passenger by any vehicle to or from his place of work shall, notwithstanding that the worker is under no obligation to his employer to travel by that vehicle, be deemed to arise out of and in the course of his employment if —

(a)   the accident would have been deemed so to have arisen had he been under such obligation, and

(b)   at the time of the accident the vehicle —
  (i) is being operated by or on behalf of his employer or some other person by whom it is provided in pursuance of arrangements made with his employer, and
  (ii) is not being operated in the ordinary sense of a public transport service.

It follows from the wording of the section that the employer must either provide or arrange for the provision of the vehicle as in the case of the hiring of a works bus. Injuries sustained by a worker whilst coming to work by means of his own transport are not covered.

Accidents Happening While Meeting an Emergency

S. 54 of the 1975 Act provides that an accident happening to a worker in or about any premises at which he is for the time being employed for the purposes of his employer's trade or business shall be deemed to arise out of and in the course of his employment if it happens while he is taking steps, on an actual or supposed emergency at those premises, to rescue, succour or protect persons who are, or are thought possibly to be, injured or imperilled, or to avert or minimise serious damage to property.

There must be a link between the emergency and the employment. Thus in one case a worker was asked to hold a window frame so that it would not fall and cause injury while a co-worker hammered a piece of wood on to it. The hammering brought down some bricks which injured the worker who was holding the frame and it was held that he was entitled to benefit (C.I. 280/49). However, in another case a civil servant, who while visiting houses on behalf of his employer, the National Assistance Board, stopped a runaway bicycle which was coming down a hill out of control, was held not entitled to benefit because the act of stopping the bicycle was not incidental to his employment (R(I) 52/54).

Accidents Caused by Another's Misconduct

S. 55 of the 1975 Act provides that a worker is entitled to benefit if he is injured by an accident which arises in the course of employment and the accident either is caused by another person's misconduct, skylarking or negligence, or by steps taken in consequence of any such misconduct, skylarking or negligence or by the behaviour or presence of an animal (including a bird, fish or insect), or is caused by or consists in the worker being struck by any object or by lightning, and the worker did not directly or indirectly induce or contribute to the happening of the accident by his conduct outside the employment or by any act not incidental to the employment.

As we have seen, a claimant recovered benefit when he suffered scalding because his employer's daughter-in-law, with whom he worked, threw boiling water over him (C.I. 51/49).

BENEFITS UNDER THE ACT

S. 50 of the 1975 Act describes industrial injuries benefits. They are set out below.

Injury Benefit

This is payable when a worker is incapable of work due to an accident or disease. It is payable during a maximum period of 26 weeks from the date of the accident or development of the disease.

Disablement Benefit

This is payable where there is loss of physical or mental faculty because of an industrial accident or disease *and* disablement is assessed at not less than 1 per cent. It is not available until the injury benefit period has ended. Where the disablement is assessed between 1 per cent but under 20 per cent it is paid as a lump sum. If the disablement is 20 per cent or more it is paid as a weekly pension.

Disablement benefit may be increased as follows:

(a) Unemployability supplement

This is an additional weekly sum payable where incapacity for work as a result of the accident or disease is likely to be permanent.

(b) Special hardship allowance

This is an additional weekly sum payable where the worker is unable to return to a regular occupation or to do work of an equivalent standard as a result of the accident or disease.

(c) Constant attendance allowance

This is an additional weekly sum payable where the person concerned is in receipt of a 100 per cent disablement pension and constant attendance is needed due to the result of accident or disease.

(d) Exceptionally severe disablement allowance

This is an additional weekly sum payable where there is entitlement to constant attendance allowance at a rate exceeding the normal maximum and the need for the attendance is likely to be permanent.

(e) Hospital treatment allowance

This is payable if the person is receiving treatment in hospital for injury or disease for which disablement benefit has been awarded.

Death Benefit

Where a worker dies as a consequence of an industrial accident or of an industrial disease, death benefit may be payable on a weekly basis to the widow, widower, children and certain dependent relatives. It may also be paid to a woman having the care of a child of the deceased.

UNEMPLOYMENT BENEFIT

This is a flat rate basic weekly sum with allowances for dependents which may be drawn for a maximum of 312 days. There is also the possibility of an additional payment called earnings related supplement.

Disqualification from Unemployment Benefit

There are certain disqualifications preventing the receipt of unemployment benefit. These are set out below.

Trade disputes

Where a person is unemployed as a result of a trade dispute at his place of employment he is disqualified from obtaining benefit, subject to certain exceptions, e.g. as where he is not participating in the trade dispute.

Misconduct

A person who has lost his job because of his misconduct, being the kind of misconduct which gives his employer the right terminate his contract (see p. 88), is not entitled to benefit.

Voluntary termination of employment

If a person leaves a job voluntarily and without just cause, there is no entitlement to benefit.

Refusing to accept alternative employment

A person who has failed to avail himself of a reasonable opportunity of obtaining suitable alternative employment or of receiving training for it, is not entitled to benefit.

Employment is not regarded as suitable if—
   (i) the situation has become vacant because of a stoppage of work due to a trade dispute, or

(ii) the employment is in the claimant's usual occupation in the district where he was last ordinarily employed, but at a lower rate of pay, or on conditions less favourable than those which he would have obtained if he were not unemployed, or than those which he would reasonably have expected to obtain, or

(iii) the employment is in his usual employment in another district at a rate of pay or on conditions less favourable than those generally observed in that district under agreements made between associations of employers and employees, or by good employers.

However, after the lapse of a reasonable period of unemployment employment will not be regarded as unsuitable merely because it is employment different in kind from the usual employment, provided that the rate of pay and conditions are not less favourable than those generally accepted in the proposed employment.

SICKNESS AND INVALIDITY BENEFIT

Weekly flat rate sickness benefit is payable to persons who are unable to work because of illness. In addition to the flat rate benefit there are allowances for dependents. Provided the contribution conditions are satisfied, sickness benefit is payable without limitation of time while unemployed through sickness.

Invalidity benefit normally replaces sickness benefit after 160 days and consists of a weekly sum payable as an invalidity pension and an invalidity allowance payable to those where incapacity began more than five years before pension age. The allowance is payable at three rates; the first if incapacity began before the age of 35, the second if it began between 35 and 44, and the third if it began between 45 and 54 for women and 45 and 59 for men.

PROCEDURE FOR MAKING CLAIMS

Where a person wishes to make a claim for benefit under the Social Security Act, 1975, e.g. sickness or unemployment benefit, the claim must in the first instance be made to a local insurance officer who may authorise payment, or refuse payment, or refer the claim to a local tribunal.

If payment is simply refused, the person claiming can appeal to a local tribunal which has three members, two non-lawyers (one drawn from a panel of persons representing employers and the self-employed, and one drawn from a panel of persons representing employees), while the third member is usually a lawyer (for example, a local solicitor) appointed by the Secretary of State to be chairman.

If the tribunal allows the appeal the insurance officer may appeal against that decision to a National Insurance Commissioner. The same right of appeal is given to the person making the claim where the tribunal does not decide in his favour. National Insurance Commissioners are appointed by the Crown from amongst barristers and solicitors of not less than ten years' standing. Decisions of the Commissioners are usually final unless there is fresh evidence which could not have been considered when the original decision was made.

8 Trade Unions

GENERALLY

Trade unions and employers' associations have a number of privileges conferred upon them by the Trade Union and Labour Relations Act, 1974 (TULRA) and so it is essential first to establish what a trade union is and what an employers' association is.

S. 28(1) of the TULRA states that a trade union is an organisation (whether permanent or temporary) which consists wholly or mainly of workers of one or more descriptions and is an organisation whose principal purposes include the regulation of relations between workers of that description or those descriptions and employers or employers' associations. In general, a trade union must not be incorporated.

It should be noted in particular that since the Act envisages *temporary* organisations, breakaway groups of workers or shop stewards who are not willing to accept the dictates of their union are within the definition and entitled to the privileges conferred on trade unions if their activities can be regarded as regulating the relationship of employer and employee.

S. 28(2) of the TULRA states that an employers' association is an organisation (whether permanent or temporary) which consists solely or mainly of employers or individual proprietors of one or more descriptions and is an organisation whose principal purposes include the regulation of relations between employers of that description or those descriptions and workers or trade unions.

The Independence of Trade Unions

Some of the privileges given to trade unions apply only if a union is independent. S. 153 of the Employment Protection (Consolidation) Act, 1978 (EPCA) states that 'independent trade union' means a trade union which —

(a) is not under the domination or control of an employer or a group of employers or of one or more employers' associations; and

(b) is not liable to interference by an employer or any such group or association (arising out of the provision of financial or material support or by any means whatsoever) tending towards such control; and in relation to a trade union, 'independent' and 'independence' shall be construed accordingly.

It is because of these provisions that a number of staff associations have failed to establish themselves as independent trade unions.

Under s. 8 of the Employment Protection Act, 1975 (EPA) a trade union may apply to the Certification Officer for a certificate that it is independent. The Certification Officer took over in 1976 the duties of the Chief Registrar of Friendly Societies in regard to trade unions, e.g. the maintenance of a list of trade unions and employers' associations and mergers of trade unions. An independent trade union (or membership thereof) carries the following main additional advantages —

(a)   only an independent trade union can refer an issue relating to the failure of an employer to recognise it to ACAS (s. 11, EPA),

(b)   an employer is obliged to disclose information necessary for collective bargaining only to an independent trade union (s. 17, EPA),

(c)   representatives of independent trade unions must be consulted on redundancies (s. 99, EPA),

(d)   officials of an independent trade union are entitled to time off for carrying out union duties or for training in aspects of industrial relations (s. 27, EPCA),

(e)   the dismissal of an employee because he is a member of or intends to join an independent trade union or has taken or proposes to take part in its activities is unfair (s. 23, EPCA).

OTHER PROVISIONS RELATING TO TRADE UNIONS AND EMPLOYERS' ASSOCIATIONS

Under s. 8 of the TULRA the Certification Officer is required to keep a list of trade unions and a list of employers' organisations. Application for inclusion on the list is made to the Certification Officer, the application being accompanied by a copy of the rules of the organisation, a list of its officers, the address of its main or head office, and the name under which it is or is to be known.

S. 10 of the TULRA imposes a duty to keep proper accounting records and under s. 11 and Sched. 2 there is a requirement to send to the Certification Officer an annual return and accounts together with a copy of the auditor's report on the accounts and a note of any changes in the officers or the address of its head or main office.

THE RELATIONSHIP BETWEEN A TRADE UNION AND ITS MEMBERS

There are two major areas which arise for consideration here.

Union Rules

When a person joins a trade union he enters into a contract, the terms of which are the rules of the union. A member has an action for a breach of those rules which causes him damage, e.g. an action for wrongful expulsion.

BONSOR v. MUSICIANS' UNION, [1955] 3 All E.R. 518:
House of Lords

Facts

The plaintiff had been a professional musician and a member of the Musicians' Union all his working life. He was expelled from the Union under a rule relating to non-payment of contributions. After expulsion he could not obtain work as a musician since the Union was a 'closed shop'. He was at one time reduced to taking employment which involved the removing of rust from Brighton Pier. He brought an action for damages against the Union on the basis that his expulsion was null and void because his branch secretary had struck his name off the register without consulting the branch committee as the Union rules required. He also asked for an injunction restraining the Union, its servants and agents from acting on the purported expulsion.

Judgment

It was held by the House of Lords that the injunction would be granted and that damages would be awarded for breach of contract. The rules of the Union constituted a contract between the members and Bonsor was entitled to recover damages for having been wrongfully expelled in breach of the rules of the Union.

Political Funds

Since the end of the last century trade unions have, in order to provide representatives of the working man in Parliament, maintained Parliamentary candidates and members of Parliament from union funds. Some members of trade unions objected to this and political funds are now controlled by the Trade Union Act, 1913 which provides that certain conditions must be fulfilled before a political fund can be set up and money from it spent on political activities. These are as follows:

(a)   the majority of the members must have passed a resolution approving political objects as objects of the union. The voting must be by secret ballot and every member must have an equal right to vote,

   (b)   the rules of the union must provide that —

      (i) payments in favour of political objects are made out of a separate fund to be called the political fund,

      (ii) any member may by giving notice be exempt from subscribing to the political fund,

      (iii) a member who does not subscribe to the political fund is not to be excluded from any benefits or placed under any disability or disadvantage compared with other members of the union, though he can be excluded from matters concerning the management of the political fund,

      (iv) contributing to the political fund is not to be a condition of admission to membership of the union.

RESTRICTIONS ON THE LEGAL LIABILITY OF TRADE UNIONS AND THEIR MEMBERS

Generally

An act which might otherwise be the basis of a legal action, e.g. inducing a breach of contract, may not be so if it is carried out by a person in contemplation of furtherance of a trade dispute.

Meaning of Trade Dispute

S. 29(1) of the TULRA states that 'trade dispute' means a dispute between employers and workers, or between workers and workers, which is connected with one or more of the following, that is to say —

   (a)   terms and conditions of employment, or the physical conditions in which any workers are required to work;

   (b)   engagement or non-engagement, or termination or suspension of employment or the duties of employment, of one or more workers;

   (c)   allocation of work or the duties of employment as between workers or groups of workers;

   (d)   matters of discipline;

   (e)   the membership or non-membership of a trade union on the part of a worker;

   (f)   facilities for officials of trade unions;

   (g)   machinery for negotiation and consultation, and other procedures relating to any of the foregoing matters, including the recognition by employers or employers' associations of the right of a trade union to represent workers in any such negotiations or consultation or in the carrying out of such procedures.

The definition of 'trade dispute' and 'worker' is wide enough to include strikes in sympathy with or to support persons in other industries. Inter-union disputes are covered. However, in all cases there must be a trade dispute either existing or in contemplation.

CONWAY v. WADE, [1909] A.C. 506: House of Lords

Facts

Conway was employed by Readhead & Sons. Wade, in order to compel Conway to pay a fine due to a trade union and to punish him for not paying it, persuaded Readhead's foreman to dismiss Conway by threats that unless Conway was dismissed the union men in Readhead's service would stop work. Conway left his employment because of this threat and suffered damage. The only defence put forward by Wade at the trial was that he was protected by previous legislation protecting him if there was a trade dispute.

Judgment

At the trial the jury found that there was no trade dispute existing or contemplated by the men, and that Wade's threats were uttered in order to compel Conway to pay a union fine and to punish him for not paying it and to prevent him from getting or obtaining employment, and they awarded Conway damages. On an appeal to the House of Lords the House of Lords also held that Wade was outside the protec-tion of the then legislation because there was no trade dispute. The legislation did not extend to a purely personal vendetta.

Meaning of Worker

'Worker' is defined by s. 30, TULRA as a person who works, normally works, or seeks work under a contract of employment, whether express, implied, written or oral. Independent contractors are 'workers' unless they provide professional services for clients so that e.g. accountants and solici-tors are excluded but a jobbing builder is included.

Those employed by Government departments are included, as are those employed by the National Health Service. The police and armed forces are excluded.

Main Areas Requiring Legal Protection

The three major civil wrongs which can occur in trade disputes and in respect of which the law gives protection to a trade union and its members are con-sidered below.

(i) Inducing a breach of contract

At common law if A persuades B to break his contract with C, then C can sue A.

LUMLEY v. GYE, (1853) 2 E. & Bl. 216: High Court

Facts

The plaintiff, who was the manager of an opera house, made a contract with a *prima donna*, Johanna Wagner, for her exclusive services for a period of time. Gye induced Johanna Wagner to break her operatic engagement with the plaintiff and sing for him.

Judgment

It was held that whatever might have been the origin of the right to sue in such cases as this, it was not now confined to actions by masters for the enticement of their servants but extended to wrongful interference with any contract of personal service.

(ii) Intimidation

If A threatens to act unlawfully against B, intending that B will act to the detriment of C, then A has committed the tort of intimidation.

ROOKES v. BARNARD, [1964] 1 All E.R. 367: House of Lords

Facts

Rookes, who was employed in the design office of BOAC, resigned from membership of his trade union. Under an agreement made in 1949 between BOAC and its employees it was provided that no lockout or strike should take place and any dispute should be referred to arbitration. This agreement was part of each contract of employment. Rookes' office was subject to a 'closed-shop' agreement and when he refused to re-join the union certain officials of the union served notice on BOAC that unless Rookes was removed they would withdraw the labour of their members and would not go to arbitration. They were thus in breach of their contract of service. As a result BOAC lawfully terminated Rookes' contract of service after giving him a much longer period of notice than the contract required. Rookes brought an action for damages against the defendants for using unlawful means to induce BOAC to terminate the contract of service with him and/or conspiring to have him dismissed by threatening BOAC with strike action if he were retained.

Judgment

The House of Lords held that on the facts the defendants had committed the tort of intimidation and that legislation then in force did not protect them since it did not cover, even in a trade dispute, the interference with a contract of service brought about by unlawful intimidation.

(iii) Civil conspiracy

Under the law relating to civil conspiracy, the courts found it necessary to regard a strike as a conspiracy to injure for which the employer could recover damages from union funds and property.

QUINN v. LEATHEM, [1901] A.C. 495: House of Lords

Facts

Quinn was the treasurer of a Belfast union of butchers' assistants. Leathem was a flesher who employed assistants who were not members of the union. Initially the union tried to persuade Leathem to dismiss his non-union assistants but he would not do so. However, he did agree to pay any demand the union might make if it would admit his assistants to membership. The union refused to admit Leathem's assistants and approached a butcher called Munroe, who often bought meat from Leathem, and threatened to call a strike of his employees unless he ceased buying meat from Leathem. Munroe complied with the request of the union and cased to buy meat from Leathem who brought an action against Quinn and other officials of the union on the ground that they had conspired together in order to injure his business.

Judgment

At the trial the jury awarded Leathem £250 damages and Quinn later appealed to the House of Lords, where the award of the jury was upheld on the basis of conspiracy by Quinn and others to damage the business of Leathem.

The Source of Protection

The TULRA gives protection to persons who commit the wrongs set out in (i), (ii) and (iii) above if there is a trade dispute. It is s. 13 which applies and this is set out in full below.

'13.—(1) An act done by a person in contemplation or furtherance of a trade dispute shall not be actionable in tort on the ground only —

    (a) that it induces another person to break a contract or interferes or induces another person to interfere with its performance; or

    (b) that it consists in his threatening that a contract (whether one to which he is a party or not) will be broken or its performance interfered with or that he will induce another person to break a contract of employment to which that other person is a party.

(2) For the avoidance of doubt it is hereby declared that an act done by a person in contemplation or furtherance of a trade dispute is not actionable in tort on the ground only that it is an interference with the trade, business or employment of another person, or with the right of another person to dispose of his capital or his labour as he wills.

(3) For the avoidance of doubt it is hereby declared that:

    (a) an act which by reason of subsection (1) or (2) above is itself not actionable;

    (b) a breach of contract in contemplation or furtherance of a trade dispute;

shall not be regarded as the doing of unlawful act or the use of unlawful means for the purpose of establishing liability in tort.

(4) An agreement or combination by two or more persons to do or procure the doing of any act in contemplation or furtherance of a trade dispute shall not be actionable in tort if the act in question is one which, if done without such agreement or combination, would not be actionable in tort.'

It will be noted that subsections (1) and (2) of s. 13 reverse or nullify the decisions in *Lumley* v. *Gye* and *Rookes* v. *Barnard*, where there is a trade dispute, and subsections (3) and (4) effect the reversal of *Quinn* v. *Leathem*.

The Trade Union and Labour Relations (Amendment) Act, 1976, s. 3 makes it clear that the statutory immunity in regard to inducing breach of contract is not confined to contracts of employment but extends e.g. to inducing breaches of contract with those who supply the employer with goods.

The activities of trade unions in industrial disputes are often also contrary to the common law of restraint of trade and criminal conspiracy. Once again, however, the TULRA in s. 2(5) and s. 3(5) and s. 13(3) provides protection during a trade dispute.

Picketing

This is covered by the TULRA, s. 15 which provides that it shall be lawful for one or more persons in contemplation or furtherance of a trade dispute to attend at or near —

(a)   a place where another person works or carries on business; or

(b)   any other place where another person happens to be, not being a place where he resides,

for the purpose only of peacefully obtaining or communicating information, or peacefully persuading any person to work or abstain from working.

S. 7 of the Conspiracy and Protection of Property Act, 1875 is also relevant and provides that every person who, with a view to compelling any other person to abstain from doing or to do any act which such other person has a legal right to do or abstain from doing wrongfully and without legal authority —

(a)   uses violence to or intimidates such other person or his wife or children or injures his property, or

(b)   persistently follows him about from place to place, or

(c)   hides any tools or clothes or other property owned or used by him, or deprives him or hinders him in the use thereof, or

(d)   watches or besets the house or other place where he resides, or works, or carries on business, or happens to be, or the approach to such house or place, or

(e)   follows him with two or more other persons in a disorderly manner in or through any street or road,

is, on conviction, liable to pay a fine not exceeding £20 or to imprisonment not exceeding three months.

It will be seen that the above provisions do not authorise the sort of picketing which has been seen in industrial disputes over the last few years. However, the police have been reluctant to arrest pickets for some of the crimes which they commit, such as breaches or threatened breaches of the peace and obstruction of traffic and of the highway. In addition, secondary picketing has become a problem. This occurs e.g. when the employees of A, who are in dispute with A, picket the factory of B where employees are not in dispute so as e.g. to cut supplies of materials to A in order to hasten a settlement of the dispute with A. The present Conservative Government's Consultative Working Paper proposes to limit the right to picket to those involved in the dispute at their own place of work and to afford protection to those not involved in the dispute who are suffering from secondary action. The working paper dismisses the possibility of making unlawful picketing a crime but proposes to give employees the right to apply to the courts for a declaration that the picketing in question is lawful or unlawful.

9 Employment and the EEC

THE INSTITUTIONS OF THE EEC

Since Britain joined the EEC it has been necessary to take into account legislation emanating from the institutions of the Community. These institutions are —

(a) *The Commission*. This consists of 13 Commissioners, France, Germany, Italy and Britain appointing two each, and other countries one each. Commissioners are required to act independently of their national governments and in the interest of the Community. The Commission initiates all major Community legislation which is placed before the Council of Ministers for enactment.

(b) *Council of Ministers*. This consists of one representative of each of the Member States. The representative is usually the Foreign Secretary but others may attend where a matter of importance in a particular area is involved, e.g. if agriculture, the Minister of Agriculture. The Council enacts legislation and generally a simple majority is required.

(c) *European Parliament (or Assembly)*. This represents the citizens of the Member States. Seats are allocated on the basis of population and there are now direct elections. The Parliament does not legislate but advises. It provides a means by which Community problems can be discussed and questions put to the Council and Commission.

EEC LEGISLATION

There are two major types of Community legislation which concern us. These are —

(a) *Regulations*, which are of general application in the Member Countries and, under Art. 189 of the Treaty of Rome in theory, become part of domestic law without Parliament needing to take cognisance of them. In practice, however, some may give rise to consequential subordinate legislation or require the repeal or amendment of existing Acts.

(b) *Directives*, which are, under Art. 189, binding in principle, but it is left to the Member Countries to decide upon the means of giving them legal and administrative effect, usually within a given time scale. In Britain this is dealt with by s. 2 of the European Communities Act, 1972, and the most common method of incorporating directives into British law will be by statutory instruments, though the UK's response to the First Directive on Company Law was included in s. 9 of the European Communities Act, 1972. Nevertheless, fundamental obligations in a directive, such as free movement of workers, which are not subject to any exceptional conditions may have immediate effect without the need for legislation in the UK. (See *Van Duyn* v. *The Home Office*, 1974, p. 32.)

THE TREATY OF ROME

The provisions of the Treaty are enforceable in the High Court under s. 2 of the European Communities Act, 1972, provided that the terms of the Treaty are sufficiently detailed to be enforced. Often the terms of the Treaty are too general to give detailed rights and it needs an English statute to give a detailed account of the rights conferred so that a court is in a position to enforce them.

THE RELATIONSHIP BETWEEN EEC LAW AND THE LEGISLATION OF MEMBER STATES

S. 2 of the European Communities Act, 1972 requires UK judges to enforce rights conferred by the Treaty and s. 3 requires them to follow decisions of the European Court. S. 2(4) of the 1972 Act deals expressly with the supremacy of Community Law by giving UK judges a rule of construction in regard to later domestic legislation. The section says that, where possible, this later domestic legislation is to be interpreted so as not to conflict with the Treaty. It does not, however, deal with the question of what is to happen if later domestic legislation is clearly wholly inconsistent with the Treaty so that no interpretation is possible or required. In such a situation it is the view of some, including Lord Denning, that it is the duty of the Courts to give priority to Community Law.

THE EUROPEAN COURT OF JUSTICE

This Court, which sits in Luxembourg, is charged with ensuring that Community Law is observed in regard to the interpretation and implementation of the Treaties. Its decisions must be accepted by the courts of Member States and there is no right of appeal. Matters before the Court are disposed of in front of all the judges. Each Member State appoints one judge so that there are nine, and the judges themselves elect the President of the Court. There is no requirement of professional law practice and the Court consists of professional judges, academic lawyers and public servants. As regards the reference of cases to the European Court by UK judges, Lord Denning laid down certain guidelines in *Bulmer* v. *Bollinger*, [1974] 2 All E.R. 1226. The main guidelines are as follows —

(i) *The time to get a ruling.* The length of time which may elapse before a ruling can be obtained from the European Court should always be borne in mind. The average length of time at present seems to be between six and nine months. It is important to prevent undue protraction of proceedings.

(ii) *The European Court must not be overloaded.* In this connection it should be borne in mind that the European Court consists of nine judges. All nine must sit on a reference from a national court and they cannot split up into divisions of three or five judges. Thus, if there are too many references, the Court would not be able to get through its work.

(iii) *The reference must be on a question of interpretation only of the Treaty.* It is a matter for the national courts to find the facts and apply the Treaty, though the way in which the national court has interpreted the Treaty can then be a matter for reference. *Bulmer's Case* also decides that the High Court and the Court of Appeal have a jurisdiction to interpret Community Law and that they are not obliged to grant a right of appeal to the European Court of Justice. However, if the case goes to the House of Lords on appeal, the House of Lords is bound to refer the matter to the European Court of Justice if either or both of the parties wishes this.

RELEVANT ARTICLES OF THE TREATY

Certain articles of the Treaty of Rome, which established the European Economic Community, are relevant to employment and are summarised below.

Freedom of Movement for Workers

Articles 48 and 49 provide that freedom of movement for workers should be secured within the Community. This, says the Articles, entails the abolition of any discrimination based on nationality between workers of the Member States as regards employment, remuneration and other conditions of work and employment. It also entails, say the Articles, the right —

(a) to accept offers of employment actually made;

(b) to move freely within the territory of Member States for this purpose;

(c) to stay in a Member State for the purpose of employment in accordance with the provisions governing the employment of nationals of that State laid down by law, regulation or administrative action;

(d) to remain in the territory of a Member State after having been employed in that State, subject to conditions which shall be embodied in implementing regulations to be drawn up by the Commission.

The above provisions apply to employment in the public services.

Article 49 deals also with particular areas in which directions should be issued or regulations made to ensure freedom of movement, e.g. by ensuring close co-operation between national employment services.

Exchange of Young Workers

Article 50 provides that the Member State shall, within the framework of a joint programme, encourage the exchange of young workers.

Social Policy

Article 117 states that the Member Countries agree upon the need to promote improved working conditions and an improved standard of living for workers. Article 118 gives the Commission the task of promoting close co-operation between Member States in the social field, particularly in matters which relate to employment, labour law and working conditions, basic and advanced vocational training, social security, prevention of occupational accidents and diseases, occupational hygiene, and the right of association and the collective bargaining between employers and workers.

Equal Pay and Holidays

Article 119 requires the Member States to ensure and maintain the application of the principle that men and women should receive equal pay for equal work, while Article 120 requires the maintenance of equivalent schemes for paid holidays.

RELEVANT REGULATIONS AND DIRECTIVES

It is not necessary in a book of this nature to consider in detail the various regulations and directives which have been made to firm up the provisions of the Treaty. There are important regulations and directives in the area of freedom of movement, equal pay, and equal treatment for women in training, promotion, access to employment and working conditions, together with redundancy and the safeguards of rights in take-overs and mergers. Many of these have already been implemented in UK statutes, such as the Sex Discrimination Act, 1975, and the Employment Protection (Consolidation) Act, 1978.

Index to Statutes

Index to Cases

General Index